Third-Year Sobriety

Third-Year Sobriety

Finding Out
Who You Really Are

GUY KETTELHACK

HAZELDEN

Hazelden
Center City, Minnesota 55012-0176
1–800–328–0094 (Toll-free U.S., Canada, and the Virgin Islands)
1–651–257–1331 (Fax)
www.hazelden.org

Library of Congress Cataloging-in-Publication Data

Kettelhack, Guy.
    Third-year sobriety : finding out who you really are / Guy
Kettelhack.
        p.   cm.
    Originally published: 1st ed. San Francisco : HarperSanFrancisco,
© 1992 (Harper sobriety series ; v. 3).
    Includes bibliographical references.
    ISBN: 978-1-56838-232-6

    1. Alcoholics—Rehabilitation—United States—Case studies.
I. Title.
HV5279.K485   1998
362.292'86—dc21   98–28443
                                                               CIP

26 25 24 23 22   11 10 9

Book design by Will H. Powers
Cover design by David Spohn
Typesetting by Stanton Publication Services, Inc.

Editor's note
The first-person stories in this book accurately reflect the feelings, experiences, and circumstances expressed by recovering individuals, but
all names, locations, and identifying details have been changed.

Contents

Author's Note

I'm a recovering alcoholic, and a writer who has grappled for some time with how to express what "recovery" means. The triumph and beauty of recovery from addiction is, to me, endlessly fascinating. Seeking to understand what goes on in recovery seems to me to be exploring what it means to become fully human.

So far, the best way I've found to convey the miraculous consciousness I find in recovery is simply to report what I hear from other recovering people. I've tried to be a kind of journalistic sponge—soaking up information, attempting to pass it on with as little interference as possible. This approach brings me one especially happy dividend: The sponge, as it soaks up information about recovery, ends up profiting as much as anyone else. The adventure of sobriety chronicled in this and other books I've done applies to *me* too. The bottom line is that I feel like a wide-eyed kid listening to what other people tell me about their recovery—as excited and grateful to have been helped by their experience, strength, and hope as I hope you will be too, reading about it in these pages. The spirit of this book can be expressed simply: *We're all in this together.*

What I hope to do here is to offer you, via the voices and insights of hundreds of recovering alcoholics and drug addicts I've listened to across the country, a rich sense of the strange, sometimes frightening, usually baffling, but ultimately wonderful adventure sobriety can mean. Whatever year, month, day, hour, or moment of sobriety you may be facing right now, you will, I hope, find strong evidence herein that you can get through it in full consciousness: You don't have to pick up a drug or a drink. That's the main testament of the people whose stories you'll read here, and the main message of hope. It's our experience that life lived consciously just about always beats life lived blindly. I hope you'll let the people in this book show you how and why, one day at a time, we've found that to be true.

Acknowledgments

Every one of the recovering men and women whose stories are chronicled in this series is owed a debt of gratitude I cannot ever hope to repay, except, perhaps, by passing on their message—that we can all live more fully, joyfully, and consciously, no matter what our "stage" of sobriety—to as wide an audience as possible. I am thankful to them, and to you, for teaching me that we can all live sober and satisfying lives.

Third-Year Sobriety

Introduction

Going Deeper: The Doubts, Discoveries, and Abundance of Third-Year Sobriety

"Nobody ever told me how to handle life when it gets better," says Janet, a recovering alcoholic with over two years' sobriety in AA. "It's like something I just heard in a meeting: Be careful of what you want—you may get it."

I met Janet for lunch in the lobby of a big midtown Manhattan office building at a time she'd set carefully: 12:15. "Now that my boss has promoted me," she said, "I want to be sure I get out after he leaves but early enough to get back before he does. He says he only feels secure when he sees me at my desk, so I try to be there whenever he's in the office. Can you imagine? Someone feeling secure because *I'm* around? Whoa—somebody changed the script!"

Until recently Janet had worked for about a year and a half as a file clerk/secretary at a major New York advertising company. "I started the job about seven months after I got sober. My first full-time job in ten years. God, was I scared." In those first months, it was amazing to Janet that she could get to work on time, keep a smiling face, answer the phone pleasantly and efficiently, go to lunch ("lunch that meant *food*, not six shots of vodka"), come back to file and type, leave and go to an AA meeting, go home to make dinner, and get to bed at a reasonable time.

"All of that was a miracle," she says. "I never realized I could have a life like this. It might have looked like nothing to some upwardly mobile, nonalcoholic friends, people I went to college with who have long since climbed career ladders into big-shot positions. But for me, after the degradation of those last years of living on welfare with no friends, my family having given up on me—the devastation and the self-hate and loneliness of those last years . . ." Janet sighs. "Let's just say that holding a job as a file clerk was just fine for somebody with as little self-esteem as I had. In fact, it was a triumph."

But what Janet faces now, in her third year of sobriety, is even more amazing to her than the discovery in her first and second years that she could get through a day without drinking. "Just because I'm showing up and using my head in some kind of consistent way, I'm doing enough of a good job that people at work are noticing. My boss, a gruff guy in his late fifties who isn't given to complimenting you just to make you feel better, decided I could help more as a think person, as he puts it, than as a secretary or file clerk. I hadn't realized how often in the past six months or the past year he'd been coming to me for advice about how to handle this or that client, or about the effectiveness of a particular ad; I certainly didn't realize I was having any influence on him. But here I am with a promotion. And the go-ahead to start working with my own clients!"

Janet takes a deep breath. "So much is kicking up for me now. I feel like I'm an impostor. I've just somehow managed to pull the wool over everybody's eyes; I'm really no good at this. It's the old feeling that I just don't deserve good things in my life. In my head I can understand that that's an old low-esteem tape I've played my whole life. And what I hear in AA tells me that I've got the choice to see life differently, to choose to adopt a positive attitude. But my self-hatred is so deeply ingrained. I have to talk about every success I'm having in my life with other recovering alcoholics, just like I have to talk about every failure. They're equally frightening to me! All of this is such new territory."

Ted, a high school English teacher with two years and three months of sobriety in NA, admits to feeling the same kind of reflexive negativity about himself, feeling that he's not deserving. But he's able to acknowledge that living with this feeling (rather than blocking it out, as he used to do, with grass and cocaine) is drawing him deeper into himself and teaching him about the roots of that negativity. "I did a Fourth Step in my first year of sobriety," he says, "but it was a real rush job. So much inventory didn't get taken. Now my discomfort even with the good stuff in my life is making me want to take a deeper look. Some things are just fine; I still manage to feel grateful for the simple, basic fact that I'm not dealing drugs, and that my life isn't the wreck that drugging made it be. The reality that I've been able to get through more than two years without picking up still astonishes me. But all this time in sobriety—going to meetings, going to work, showing up for just about everything in my life—has been kind of sweeping the house, clearing up a lot of refuse. What's left is the bare furniture and walls. And some of what I'm seeing, now that so much has been cleared away, is disturbing. Not only my old self-hate, which still seems to be thriving, but the ways that I'm drawn to escape my feelings even in sobriety. I've got some real problems with debt, sex, and ice cream. Money, sex with as many partners as I can find, and stuffing myself with food until I can't taste it anymore: I know these are all as addictive as drugs ever were. They're not killing me like drugs—at least not yet—but they're connected to the same root.

"I've gotten through more than two years of sobriety, so I know a little more about who I am sober. At first I was just so glad not to be strung out all the time; the relief of physical sobriety, once I got over my cocaine withdrawal, was enough to make me feel better about myself. But now that the house has been cleaned up a bit, I see that it needs some renovations. Maybe some major renovations. I can't get away from this feeling that I've got to take a closer look at myself. Not out of idle curiosity. Out of pain. The pain of realizing that I'm still besieged by some kind of *hunger*, a hunger that has driven me my whole life, and that I haven't been able to eradicate by simply giving up drugs. I used to think that the purpose of sobriety was to blot out that hunger, that working the program was a way for me to escape hunger like I used to escape it through drugs. But now I'm getting a different idea. Not only that maybe the hunger won't ever go away—which, God knows, it hasn't so far!—but that it may not even be the real problem. The problem is how I *react* to it."

Much of what Janet and Ted are facing is the result of a common discovery many people make in the third year of their recovery: There are no simple answers, prizes, gold stars, diplomas, or other signs that you've completed one or another stage of sobriety. Not that the Twelve Steps don't offer some concrete suggestions; doing the Steps can bring feelings of real accomplishment. It's common to feel, for example, that once you've done the Fourth and Fifth Steps (taking a fearless moral inventory of yourself and then revealing to your "Higher Power" and another person what you've found) you've completed a rite of passage. But generally, the experience of life in sobriety isn't a matter of hopping from one definite peak to another. It has a much more ongoing quality. As Ted puts it, "I keep waking up, and there's always another day to fill. When I did drugs, I think I expected somehow that my life would turn out to be a novel, with a clear plot, one adventure after another, all leading up to some great climax—and then I'd die. Just the idea of moment after moment of being conscious, with no clear milestones, no clear idea of what the next destination will be—boy, sometimes I think if I didn't have the support and insight that NA gives me, I'd slit my wrists!"

Now that you've managed to get through two years of sobriety, you know what it feels like to go through day after day, and now year after year, without getting blitzed. This is a rich and varied feeling for every recovering person I've listened to. "I never knew what gratitude was before," Janet says. "It never occurred to me I could be grateful simply to be alive. Now I know what that means, what it feels like, and how healing the feeling can be." However, feelings about recovery can also include exasperation at the things in your life, the attitudes and circumstances, that haven't changed, or that may even seem to have gotten worse.

The result of these conflicting feelings is often that you're drawn more deeply into yourself; living consciously seems to make you want to find out more about who you really are. And it's not, as Ted said, a matter of idle curiosity. Commonly, your own pain at feeling stuck in one or more areas of sobriety becomes a powerful motivation to go further and deeper into yourself, so that you have hope of working with what you find to build a better life. Not, heaven knows, that any of this is easy.

The Hard Work of Being Conscious

"Being conscious all the time is a bitch," says Greg, who has just over two years of sobriety. "It's hard work to stay awake. I can't tell you how many times I've nodded off at AA meetings. But when I look at why I'm nodding off, it's almost always more than tiredness. It's because I don't want to face what people are talking about. Especially when people talk about taking responsibility for their lives. It's easy to be crazy, and decide you're just not accountable for your actions. Or to throw up your hands and say, 'Screw it!' I think if I had one rallying cry when I drank it was 'Leave me alone!' Life was always *bothering* me. If I had to do anything, it was too much. Sometimes I still feel that way. I guess I realize now that these are growing pains—at least, that's what my sponsor suggests—and that I'm like an ornery kid who's just been awakened by his mother and told he has to get up and go to school. I get a bad case of the don't-wanna's. I want to sleep. I want to check out. That's the first impulse I've always got. But now that I'm not drinking anymore, I've lost my main way of checking out. I'm just more *awake* than I ever was before in my life. And a lot of times it's a bitch. When I finally surrender to the fact that it is time to get up, it can be pretty good. If sobriety were only a bitch, I'd be out there drinking again. But it's more than that: It's an adventure. When I manage to keep my eyes open, I'm usually pretty astonished by what I see. The world's a lot more interesting and colorful than it ever used to be. Whenever I want to be entertained, all I've got to do is open my eyes, and there life is, in all its nutty, unpredictable wonder. When I allow myself to be sober (and it does seem to take *allowing*, not willing or force) I see that I'm part of what I'm watching, I'm part of the ongoing parade. The bottom line is, it's better being alive than being dead—or at least that's what it feels like when I can find the energy to keep going. But my first reflex is still to go to sleep, to block it all out."

A lot of people drop out of AA and NA and other Twelve Step groups after two or three years for precisely this reason. It's hard to be conscious when you've spent so much of your life trying to avoid being conscious. You're not always convinced that the rewards sobriety promises are worth the effort. Many people simply get bored with meetings after about two years. "Why do they keep repeating the same damned things?" a nurse's aide, Kitty, asked. "I'm so sick of hearing the same jargon over and over again. And it's getting in the way of my life! Sometimes I think AA ought to be called Underachievers Anonymous, given all the people I listen to who do nothing but go to meetings, who've made the program their whole life. When do they ever go out and do anything? Okay, I know what it was like for me in my first year or so. All I could do was get myself to a meeting. So maybe

I'm losing sight of what that felt like—how hard it was simply to get through the day without picking up. But I'm still uncomfortable. I've got things to do, a life to live! I can't spend all my time talking about alcoholism."

These doubts and feelings of exasperation and frustration are not only normal, they're endemic. A lot of recovering people go through serious periods of doubt about what they hear at Twelve Step meetings. But these same doubts and frustrations can turn out to be opportunities rather than just pains in the you-know-what. A few weeks after she complained about the repetition in AA, Kitty has decided to change the meetings she goes to and to talk to new people about what her experience in recovery has been. "It was *because* I was disgruntled and unhappy with my recovery that I was able to go further," she says. "It's funny—now I really know what Bill W. meant when he said 'pain is the touchstone of progress.' After all, it was my pain that finally got me to want to stop drinking, wasn't it? It seems to be the same thing now: When I hurt, it becomes a signal that something needs looking at, that I've got the opportunity to look at it."

Pain hurts. But many third-year recoverers tell me they have gained a greater understanding of how to deal with this hurt. Learning to see pain as a signal, as an opportunity to grow, is a major and important task for everyone in recovery, no matter how much time we have; but it does seem to be common for people in their third year of sobriety to confront this task with a special urgency. When, as for Janet, the externals of your life take a turn for the better but you're as baffled and disturbed by this as you want to be elated, or when they don't take a turn for the better and you wonder what you're doing wrong; when you begin to see that the process of sobriety you've embarked on is a lifelong one, not a sort of diploma course from which you can graduate and move on; when you begin to see and be bothered by certain behaviors that you feel are as addictive as the one you've turned to a Twelve Step program to give up, you are in the company of a vast majority of third-year recoverers.

Facing all of these questions and feelings boils down to something relatively simple. What you're exploring is finding out who you really are. It's a process for which you've been preparing all along in sobriety, whether you knew it or not. Like Ted, who tells about the clearing and renovation he underwent in his first two years, you have been renovating your own "house." The clarity this clearing process affords isn't always comfortable, but in many third-year recoverers' experience, it can be fascinating and rewarding. Looking at your fears, at the ways in which you approach the prospect of work and relationships, at other addictions you feel you can no longer ignore, and finally at what recovery means to you now that you've managed to complete more than two years of it—all of this constitutes the territory so many people travel in their third year of recovery. Third-year recoverers have rich stories to tell about self-discovery.

Ted says one realization he's had is simple: "Things *do* pass. But things also arrive. Dealing with both those realities takes all the help I can get." Facing life's arrivals and passages in sobriety has surprises and rewards that many recovering men and women are in the active process of exploring, surprises and rewards that seem to be available to anyone who sticks with the hard work of being "conscious." Is the effort worth it? There is nothing *more* worth it than finding out about who you really are. The men and women in this book make the case for that themselves.

one

Rewards:
A New System

"What happens to my dreams now?" Kenneth's expression and tone are full of a challenge to which he knows there is no easy answer. "What happens to all the plans I had, what I was going to do and be when I'm forty, fifty, sixty? Hell, nobody in my family ever died before the age of eighty-five. I planned to play the wise old man someday, with two dozen brilliant novels behind me, happily ensconced in some elite college professorship, deigning to give interviews when I was in the mood. . . ." Kenneth smiles at his mock arrogance. Then his smile cools. "I try not to feel self-pity, but it's hard. I'm only thirty-five."

Kenneth has been off drugs and alcohol for nearly two and a half years. He's proud of this, as well as of the fact that he's managed to publish two short stories in literary journals over the past couple of years. "When I drank and drugged," he says, "I was an 'if only' writer. If only they realized what a genius I was. If only someone would commission me to write a slim, perfect novel, offering me a high six-figure advance for the privilege of publishing it. If only I had the environment I deserved to have—the right apartment, the right lover, the right friends—so that I *could* write a slim, perfect novel. If only I had gone to an expensive, prestigious, elitist college so that I could have made the right connections . . ."

"Now," Kenneth says, "I'm sober. And I'm actually writing and, even more amazing, getting published. For a while my dreams didn't seem so crazy or distant anymore. What they told me in AA and NA seemed to be true: If you waited long enough, the miracle would happen. When I got the news that my first story had been accepted, you couldn't have found a more grateful recovering addict. But I hadn't bargained for the other news. . . ." Kenneth hadn't bargained for the results of an HIV test and a subsequent checkup: He tested positive for the AIDS virus and had begun to develop the pneumonia known as PCP that signals the onset of AIDS. "Why did I wait so long to get tested?" he rails at himself. "Something inside me knew I was sick, but I couldn't bear to face it. I mean, I'd accomplished the astonishing feat of getting sober. Surely that was enough to save my life, make everything else all better. At least that's what I told myself. But now . . ."

Kenneth says he feels as if the earth has been knocked out from under him. "It isn't even that I'm that afraid of dying," he says. "And anyway, I try not to think of this as a disease to die from, but rather as something to live with, something I will live with as long as I can. But then I think to myself, get real. Statistics are damned grim. It's unlikely that I'll be around in ten years. The whole person I'd fantasized myself turning into—now there's just this huge black void in front of me. I'm already so advanced in this damned disease. How much time have I got, really? Five years? Two years? One? What the hell happened to my future? And what the hell does sobriety mean in the midst of all this? Why bother keeping sober? Why not just throw myself into one last, huge self-destructive binge and get it over with now?"

When Kenneth feels like this, he says, "I try to remember that all sobriety has ever promised me was one day at a time. That's the bedrock of recovery for me—all I've got is now. But it's one thing to tell yourself that when you haven't been branded with this disease, a disease that makes any long-term plans pretty much unthinkable. And then I try to remember, well, aren't my alcoholism and drug addiction life-threatening illnesses too? I've learned to live with them, haven't I? Isn't there something from all this that I can apply to this new terminal illness?"

Perhaps the most powerful examples of sobriety for me have been men and women who, like Kenneth, have had to rethink their dreams, aspirations, and goals because they faced what was very likely the imminent end of their lives. Whether they've battled AIDS, cancer, heart disease, or any other life-threatening illness, so many recovering people have been able to live with affliction in remarkable ways, ways that have a special bearing on one of the main messages of recovery. It seems that every recovering person who sticks with sobriety eventually gets this message: Sobriety is an inside job. To get the most out of recovery, you need to look *in*, not out.

This is a lesson many people in their third year of sobriety learn as the result of their own experience. Living sober for over two years, you have data now you didn't have before. You learn that it's possible to get through life without escaping through alcohol and drugs. You gain a new sense of what life might be about, a sense that's quite different from the acquisitive goals ("Now that I'm sober I'll have a great body, job, income, lover, house, car . . .") you may have had before. Kenneth slammed into this realization more dramatically than many of us do: With the length of his life called into serious question, he realized that the rewards of living a sober life might turn out to be very different from what he once expected.

"Instead of seeing myself in terms of outer achievements, the praise and money and great life I was going to have as a successful writer," he says, "I'm starting to see what I'm getting from sobriety in terms of serenity and self-knowledge. At the best times, I can see that sobriety has never been about getting things in the external world. It's about changing who you are inside so that your external world will sort of distill out and take care of itself. In short, it's about trusting that what's happening in some sense *needs* to happen—the spiritual idea that I'm being taken care of even when I can't believe, from my 'externals,' that could possibly be true."

The ability to exercise this kind of faith in the face of an illness such as AIDS is one of the phenomenal rewards of sobriety Kenneth never anticipated. "I didn't realize the miracle could be so miraculous," he says. "Sometimes I feel so plugged in, so helped by what I'm learning in recovery from meetings and friends and my sponsor, from the literature I read, and from some source that is fueling all of this—I guess it's God—I can be so nurtured by all of this that I experience a complete peace. A complete self-acceptance. It's wonderful. A lot of the time it's the only thing that keeps me going."

Kenneth says this state of peace, like every other feeling in sobriety, "comes and goes. Sometimes I still panic. Sometimes I still rail at fate. But I can always return to the moment I'm in right now. There's always something productive I can do for myself right now. Thank God I've still got enough strength to write. I'm writing some true-life accounts of what I'm going through, and getting them published, which has helped other people. They've written and called to tell me they've been helped. No one could have prepared me for this—that I could help other people while I deal with this disease. And I go to all kinds of support groups, both in and out of AA and NA, that offer me help too. You can live life fully, one moment at a time, whether or not you've been told you're dying." Kenneth pauses for a moment. "And the truth is, I'm not dying now. I'm living. And that's the only thing I have to concentrate on: living, as consciously as I can, for as long as I can. The rest is out of my hands."

Not all of us find ourselves facing life-and-death issues with this kind of urgency. But all recovering people combat a life-threatening illness: addiction. The message Kenneth offers is very healing to anyone who faces life in recovery. It seems clear that the rewards of taking this message to heart have more to do with what goes on inside us than what happens outside.

Assessing "Success" in Sobriety

Sobriety isn't a monklike eternity of self-sacrifice and deprivation, a sort of punishment for not being able to drink or drug. If it were, few of us would manage to keep from drinking and drugging for any length of time; if it made us so miserable, what inducement would we have to keep it up? The Twelve Step program promise of becoming "happy, joyous, and free" is a potent one. I haven't met recovering people who don't admit to wanting a comfortable, enjoyable, happy, abundant, fulfilling, successful life. Wanting to succeed in these terms is a common and laudable goal.

By the third year, it's equally clear to most recovering people that the chances of living this or any other kind of life depend on whether they can maintain their sobriety, which means not drinking or doing drugs. "I have nothing without my sobriety," says Elizabeth, a thirty-two-year-old single mother with two daughters aged six and nine. "I'll never forget when Gail, my older daughter, started first grade and made friends whose parents sometimes invite her over after school for milk and cookies. Gail couldn't believe how clean her friend's houses were, how nice they smelled, how kind the grown-ups were. She was so used to being yelled at, so used to food rotting in the sink, so used to finding her mother passed out on the couch when she came home from school." Elizabeth is on the verge of tears, so pained is she by the memory of her own past behavior. "It's one thing to have an abusive mother," she says. "My mother was a drunk too, and she made my life hell when I was a kid. But it's another thing to realize you're *being* an abusive mother. I've got a lot of amends to make."

In the twenty-five months that Elizabeth has been sober,

some of the externals of her life have gotten better. "I'm not the slob I used to be," she says. "I mean, I still hate to clean things up, but now that I'm not drunk half the time, messes bother me as much as they bother the kids. So I'm better at running the house simply because I'm more awake for it. And I manage money a little better too. I divorced my husband when Lynn was two and Gail was five. It was one of those classic lipstick-on-the-collar routines: He was having an affair with his secretary. Self-righteously, and on the strength of half a bottle of scotch, I told him to get out and stay out. The courts took over from then on, and he's actually been good about sending alimony. Now that the checks don't go for booze anymore—they go for food and clothes—my life is simply more manageable in that regard too."

But apart from these basics, Elizabeth says, "My life hasn't really changed that much. I mean, I'm still single, I still don't have a job, and I still feel like I'm doomed to be a housewife till the end of my days. I'd like so much to do something creative. I've got some talent in art, and I thought maybe I could be a teacher's aide in an art class, or work with kids at the local YMCA on after-school art projects. But I can't seem to get it together. I don't have any experience, or the right kind of education. Who would take me on? And I've got the kids to take care of, anyway. As it is I can barely afford a baby-sitter now and then when I take myself out to a movie. Since I can't imagine getting a job that wasn't a volunteer thing, how could I afford it time- or money-wise?

"Sometimes I get terribly depressed about this. True, sobriety has cleared up a lot in my life. I'm just more present than I used to be. My kids don't wince when they see me, like they used to. But life has to be more than a cleaner kitchen or giving my kids a hot breakfast. Life has to be more than just getting through the day. Where's my piece of the pie? I used to feel I didn't deserve anything; I know that's pretty classic for recovering addicts and alcoholics. I went to a social worker who was connected to the alcoholism program I was in when I was first sober, and it was clear to me, talking to her, that the big problem was self-esteem. Like, I didn't have any. But now that's giving way to something else: anger and frustration. Okay, I'm starting to think that maybe I do deserve more than I've got. But what? And how do I get it?"

Even people whose lives do make a more dramatic external turn-around than Elizabeth's can have trouble dealing with it. Success, as conventually measured by the world, can turn out to be very unwieldy. As much as you may have striven for it, achieving it can have some unwelcome effects. "I know I'm stereotyping," says Dennis, a forty-four-year-old Vietnam veteran, "but I've always been convinced that my alcoholism, verbal gifts, and entrenched melancholy nature are my Irish heritage." He recently sold, for a substantial sum, a screenplay based on his experience after returning from the war. "I never dreamed of getting that kind of money," he says. "I remember a few years back being asked by a director friend of mine to join him out at the end of Long Island in one of the Hampton's—South or East, I can't remember, I was too drunk. I'd worked on a few low-budget screenplays with artistic pretensions. I was broke but felt terribly superior. The party was in the house of some big-shot actor, who was renting it for the season. For the whole weekend I huddled glowering in the corner, taking pulls out of a bottle of whiskey. How much I hated all those pumped-up egos striding around me! What posturing, arrogant jerks I thought they all were! But, of course, not so secretly, I was envious as hell. Why couldn't I have the life they had? I had all the talent they did, didn't I? Why couldn't I get any of the breaks?"

When Dennis got sober and finally got his break, he says, "The shock nearly knocked me over. I don't know how to explain what happened. I stood at the window of my tenement apartment in the South Bronx and looked out. It was gray, miserable, raining. It was as if, somehow, I sucked all the grayness into me, all that wet, gray misery. And I cried. With the letter in my hand that told me I was now a rich, successful Hollywood screenwriter, I stood there and cried like a baby. It wasn't exactly that I was sad. It's just that I felt so much stress. I couldn't imagine how to get rid of it. It's a wonder, now that I think of it, that it didn't occur to me to drink. But that's a lie; of course it occurred to me. The option of taking a drink always occurs to me—I'm an alcoholic through and through. But the amazing thing was that I decided it really wasn't an option, or at least not one I wanted to take. I'd been sober for more than two years, and the letter in my hand was evidence of that miracle. I wasn't going to throw it all away by picking up a drink.

"But what was I holding on to? What was this success, after all? Was it really something I wanted? Questions tumbled in about who I am, what I really want out of life—all those big questions. But the real thing was, I was afraid. Scared out of my wits. Someone had acknowledged me. Someone had told me that what I did was *wonderful*. Not just good—this was Hollywood, after all, and hyberbole is what they eat for breakfast. I had written something moving, real, beautiful, stunning, wonderful. Those were the adjectives they used. This couldn't register. I couldn't let the information in. Because, no, they didn't know, it was a fluke, it really wasn't so good. They were making a mistake. It was all somehow a mistake."

Dennis calms down after this rush of words. "What sobriety I've managed to achieve *has* helped me, though. Because it teaches me that all I ever have a chance of directing is my own behavior. And because I'd recently done that fearless moral inventory in a Fourth Step, something else was clear too. My sponsor made sure I wrote down the good stuff as well as what I felt was bad. And I realized, as I allowed all those negative voices inside me to fade, those voices telling me I was no good and it was all a mistake, I realized that, in sobriety, I'd managed to make some pretty rational and forward-looking moves in the past two years. I'd worked on this screenplay for a year and a half. I'd cultivated the contacts I had on the West Coast to the point where I knew who to send it to. I'd done some spadework. What was happening to me hadn't come from nowhere. It was the Hollywood company's decision to buy what I'd written; it wasn't my decision. If *they* decided what I'd written was good, what business was it of mine to argue? That's what they were in the business of doing—deciding such things.

"I guess what I'm saying is that, in recovery, I'm finally able to better sort out what I have power over and what I don't. And when I realize this, I let a miracle in—not just the miracle of someone buying my screenplay for a lot of money, but the miracle of my having been able to take an action and leave the result up to my Higher Power. When I realize that what happened to me wasn't entirely the result of my own machinations, of pulling strings, of pushing something through completely on my own, I should let go of it. What was happening was happening for a lot of reasons, most of which had nothing to do with my will. So I could begin to accept my success as a gift, something I'd had a hand in creating, but something that was also coming to me from outside myself. Like sobriety, it was something that came because I was receptive to it, and maybe even because I was ready to handle it. It's like that Zen Buddhist idea that the teacher appears when the student is ready. Well, maybe this bit of success was appearing because something in the Great Beyond knew I was ready to handle it. I don't know that I could have handled it any earlier. I don't know that it wouldn't have sent me out of the room right to the liquor store."

This idea of turning it over, which we often hear is synonymous with the Third Step, "Made a decision to turn our will and our lives over to the care of God *as we understood Him*," is especially useful and welcome when it comes to questions about success. It may seem strange at first to hear that Dennis had as hard a time dealing with his external good fortune as Elizabeth has dealing with what she perceives as her own lack of it. But many of the same fears and self-doubts afflict us no matter what our outward success status may be.

Allowing Externals to "Distill Out"

Kenneth touched on something essential when he said, "It's about changing who you are inside so that your external world will sort of distill out and take care of itself." A lot of people in their third year of sobriety begin to appreciate this change. "It's really hitting me," says Jacqueline, a woman from Montreal in her mid-twenties who has over two years in NA and AA, "that certain causes have certain effects, that my actions have consequences. When I moved from Montreal to California six years ago, it was like it didn't happen in reality, or it happened to some cartoon character who wasn't really me. I did everything on whim. I had some money I inherited from my grandmother, but I had no idea of saving it, or using it to make my life better. All I knew to do with it was spend it on alcohol and drugs. Suddenly I was in San Francisco. When I was drinking and drugging, I was like a puppet; my limbs would sort of jerk this way and that, with no real connection to *me*. Rules that applied to other people didn't apply to me. And, my God, the things I got away with! It's amazing the nerve I had as an active addict—I won't call it courage, because it's really just drugs-and-booze–inspired stupid nerve. Someone said, hey, pick up some good dope in Mexico and bring it back, will you? So he gives me money and I go down there and all but stuff my pockets and luggage with it and walk through customs as if I were Margaret Thatcher or somebody and nobody stops me! I did things like that all the time. Took incredible risks. But somehow, something kept saving me. Or even when the cops did pick me up, I could always flirt or lie or maneuver my way out of it. It didn't even occur to me that what I was choosing to do was killing me. And anyway, who cared about that? My only agenda was to get high and live on the edge."

Jacqueline began to try to get sober after she woke up one morning in a bathtub full of tepid water, stained pink with blood. "I'd tried to slit my wrists," she says. "But even that didn't work. I think I did it on a dare. I can't really remember. But seeing myself wrecked in that bathtub got to me. I began to acknowledge that I was really miserable. And that maybe I needed help." She says that when she first tried to get sober—"I gave it a number of tries, and was a dismal failure for about three years"—what bothered her most about AA and NA meetings was the spoken and unspoken idea that, although we were supposed to be "powerless" over our addictions, we were still responsible for our actions. "I used to think, how could that be? I mean, wasn't surrender the whole thing about sobriety? Wasn't some Great White Father in the Sky supposed to reach down and point you in the right direction, take care of you? Where was the great spiritual force I was supposed to be feeling, and depending on for strength and guidance?" No such blindingly clear guidance ever came to Jacqueline, and she never was able, as she says, "to put cause and effect together. I still couldn't get that it was my own behavior that was getting me into trouble. And beneath that, my attitudes. Yes, I'm powerless over drugs and alcohol—get me near the stuff, and I'm off to the races. But it took some time before I realized that certain circumstances that I (and nobody else) kept putting myself in—people, places, and things—always triggered me to pick up again. Finally it began to dawn on me that maybe there was something I *could* control. And, more than that, that certain attitudes and behaviors always, without fail, led to certain outcomes. In other words, what I felt and did had an effect on me, the world, and other people."

This has been a profound realization for Jacqueline, as it is for most of the rest of us. We *do* have an effect on the world. What we do does count. We're not exceptions to the rules: the laws of gravity affect *us* too. "I think this was my biggest stumbling block, not being able to see that my actions had consequences. It's really what kept me from getting sober: For so long I simply couldn't accept that I was putting myself near drugs and alcohol, which kept me going back out and losing control of my life. But now that I'm able to accept this cause-and-effect idea—that all of my actions have real consequences—it's turned into the source of my greatest insights."

What are some of these insights?

"I'm starting to see that my outer world is pretty much a direct reflection of my inner one. This works in simple ways. When I feel confused and lazy and impatient and unhappy with myself, I let my apartment turn into a pigsty. But when I start to feel better about myself, I clean things up. It's the same thing with how I look. If I feel like a monster, I look and act like a monster. If I feel like a relatively decent human being, I look and act like one. They say this disease we've got is a disease of the attitudes. Boy, is it. Everything I feel inside me keeps manifesting back up here at the surface."

Jacqueline expands on one of the revelations this principle has brought to her: "Once I realized that A does lead to B, and B does lead to C, once I realized that there are certain predictable domino effects in life, I found I was discovering what I had power over in my life, in more aspects of it than I'd ever dreamed. I'd bummed around for all of my late teens and twenties, dropping in and out of all sorts of progressive schools, learning almost nothing except how to get high, so I'd really never done anything. But then, in my second year of sobriety, I started to take cooking lessons. I'd always had the idea that I'd like to open my own restaurant, a high-class, limited menu, tiny exclusive place, with me directing the cooking. And now I was actually doing something about it—at any rate, finding out if cooking was a pipe dream or something I really wanted to do professionally. But the most amazing thing I learned wasn't cooking technique. It was that I could apply the principles I was learning in the program to the rest of my life, including cooking! First things first, easy does it, one day at a time—it all worked to help me keep going even when I messed up or couldn't get something right, which happened a lot. Maybe the biggest lesson boiled down to taking an action and leaving the results up to God. Or at least to the state of the oven. It meant keeping the focus on the moment, on what you were doing, not on how it would turn out or what other people would think of it. I found that the discipline I'd learned in staying away from drugs and alcohol carried over to my cooking. I sometimes turned into a raving perfectionistic monster, or at least until I remembered to 'turn it over,' which meant my will as well as the flour dough." Jacqueline giggles: "I gotta lighten up sometimes, you know? I'm seeing that while you can't predict or control the results of anything, you can pour a lot of energy into your own part in producing those results. And it can be fun—it's an adventure!"

Not that everything is fun, or the product of a predictable domino effect. "My father died six months ago," Jacqueline says. "It was terrible. I hadn't spoken to him since the last time I'd left home, back when I was about nineteen. He was this big respected conservative attorney, a pillar of the community, and publicly he'd have nothing to do with his renegade daughter—me. It was only after he died that my mother told me that the money she'd sent me from time to time had come from him—not from her, like I'd thought. I couldn't believe he cared enough to do that. And now I feel so awful that I wasn't able to talk to him before he died, to let him know I was better. One friend of mine in the program says you can make amends even to people who aren't around anymore. If I ask my Higher Power for forgiveness, or even forgive myself for the hurt I caused him, maybe, spiritually, the message will somehow get to my father, wherever he is."

Jacqueline's realization that we're simultaneously powerless over much in our lives *and* responsible for our own actions is one of the many paradoxes of sobriety. Sober life is often a matter of balancing what appear to be opposites. "The Serenity Prayer helps," Jacqueline says. "It seems the whole deal is to sort out what I have power over and what I don't, and, as the prayer says, to find the wisdom to know the difference. A lot of times, what I discover I don't have power over is terribly painful. I can't bring my father back. But I'm told I don't have to feel guilty about it. Concentrating on living my life productively right now is all I can do. And when I do concentrate on that, it seems to have a ripple effect. It's that passage from the inner me to the outer me I talked about: The externals of my life get better as I learn to feel better about myself. People respond more warmly and openly to me as I become more open and warmer myself.

"The trick is to keep myself from projecting what the results of my actions will be—something I'm still pretty lousy at. But sometimes it's amazing. When I am able to let go of the outcome, the outcome really takes care of itself. I don't have to worry so much. I even begin to feel like I'm being *led*, sometimes. It's not blaring trumpets or anything. It's something quiet, a kind of soft inner urging that tells me what I might want to think about doing next. Something's tugging me along. All I've got to do, most times, is quiet down enough to be receptive to it."

When You Get What You Think You Don't Want

The externals that distill out in our lives aren't always the ones we'd choose for ourselves. Elizabeth, the single mother who feels she's at square one after two years of sobriety, still hasn't found the creative calling she'd hoped to get by now. Whatever gestation period is going on, it's slower than she'd have arranged for herself. This is the case for many of us. While many recovering people in the third year experience a breakthrough about direction—perhaps with a dramatic improvement in income or job or response from the world—it's just as common to feel your progress is stuck in the mud.

Burt had his heart set on being a sculptor. He went to a midwestern state university on an art scholarship; this was unusual for a school that normally meted out its scholarships to football players. Burt himself looks a bit like a football player—a big guy, the kind you'd expect to see in a beer commercial more than in an art museum. The beer connection is apt enough. Burt, by his own admission, "loved the stuff. I was going to be one of those real men artists. You know, like Jackson Pollock, getting drunk, getting into brawls in seedy dives—the whole bit. And I was going to be a genius. Hell, by my lights, I already *was* a genius." Certainly when Burt was in his teens and early twenties, the world seemed to accommodate the image of himself he wanted to project. "People looked up to me in college," he says. "I was an artist who looked like a jock. And I was a jovial drunk. I was pretty popular."

The pattern set in school continued for about the next fifteen years. "I'd spend hours in the studio, like I was in a trance, working on this or that metal assemblage or three-dimensional collage, or chiseling away at stone. I didn't drink when I worked, at least not back in school and for the first few years afterward. I'd wait till I was done with a day's work, then I'd take Polaroid pictures of it to study what I'd done. I used to put it that way, but 'study' really meant obsess. I'd take these pictures to my room, start chugging some bourbon out of the bottle, and let my imagination run wild. By the time the pictures started to get blurry— about three-quarters of the way through the bottle—I was a Nobel Prize–winning, impossibly rich, incredibly sexy genius, and the world was just waiting to pay me homage. The actual world I was in, however, amounted to a succession of Irish drinking holes. I'd start out at the ones with singles bar pretensions— you know, like my real reason for going out was to pick up a woman. But the drunker I got, the lower and more down-and-out the bars got, till I was at some pretty dangerous places by the end. Sinkholes full of people whose idea of fun was knifing you after you passed out on the street. I had my share of fights in these places. Sometimes I imagined I was in some great dark movie about a tortured artist trying to find his soul among the real people or something."

Before long Burt's drinking had pretty much crowded out any art work. "After college, I managed to get a grant from some state arts agency. After that I picked up some freelance teaching jobs. I prided myself on supporting myself as an artist. But drinking pretty much erased everything. I wouldn't show up for appointments, so I lost all my students and, finally, all my contacts. Sometimes in a drunken rage I'd call up one of my old art professors and rail away at him: Why didn't the world appreciate what a genius I was? Soon nobody was taking my calls. I learned later that everybody had written me off as a sad case. Everybody kept expecting me to kick off, I think. Just a matter of time before I got knifed or drank myself to death."

The turning point for Burt came one night after about six hours of boozing in one of the slightly classier bars in town, an indulgence he'd funded by stealing money from an ex-lover's apartment to which he still had a key. "I managed to beg, borrow, and steal enough to keep getting drunk and pay a little rent. But something was eating away at me. I guess I knew my life was getting out of control. Basically I blamed it on the company I was keeping. Bunch of psycho down-and-out drunks. So I made myself stay in this nicer, more upscale place, a singles bar, to see if I could connect with someone who could really understand me. That's when I met Cristina."

Cristina was a woman in her late thirties who, Burt says, "smelled of patchouli, had long blond hair that she kept in a braid, and wore a tie-dyed dress. Being with her was like being in a time warp, back to some kind of weird hippie past. It felt like 1971 all over again. I convinced her I was a brilliant misunderstood artist—my usual line with women—and she went for it, the whole nine yards." After the bar closed, Burt went with her to her dark, drape-hung, incense-scented apartment. Strangely, he says, "I wasn't that drunk. Sometimes this happened to me. I'd down incredible amounts of booze and I just couldn't get high. Other times I'd black out after two or three drinks. But this was one of the nights when it just wasn't working. Anyway, I was sitting on the floor on some kind of huge pillow, and she put on an early Joni Mitchell album. It felt like I was in college again or something. Anyway, I heard this line in one of the Joni Mitchell songs:

Everybody's saying that hell's the hippest way to go—
Well, I don't think so . . .

And something in me snapped. Maybe hell *wasn't* the way to go. Maybe I'd been wrong, really, badly *wrong* about what I was do-ing to myself. It was like, in that moment, all the air went out of me, in a kind of long, slow, whoosh of surrender. I'd had it. Cristina came out of her bedroom wearing a ratty terry-cloth robe. She looked so sad and bleak standing there, her eyes dark and needy, like a child somehow. She lit a joint and offered it to me. I didn't take it. All I knew was, I had to get out of there. I had to get—where? I didn't know that either. I just had to get out. Hell was no longer the hippest way to go. That's what kept run-ning again and again in my head. Hell wasn't the way to go. Not anymore. I felt complete surrender. I'd *had* it."

However, Burt hadn't lost all his grandiose views of himself. "At first I had no idea who to call. I knew I needed help. So I de-cided—I guess I was more drunk that I thought—to call the top. If I was going to get help, it was going to have to come from the best source possible. Who would that be? Of course! The World Health Organization of the United Nations." He guffaws. "I'm not kidding. I had the phone credit card number of another ex-lover—boy, the people I ripped off!—and I dialed New York, and actually got through to the UN. Even more amazing, I got this Austrian person, I think that was her accent, who I now think might have been in the program herself. After hearing my tale of depression and woe, she gently suggested that maybe I should call AA."

Burt pauses. "Higher Powers work in mysterious ways," he says, smiling. "I don't know how may other people can say the UN got them sober. Anyway, I was ready for sobriety. It came to me because I needed it, was starving for it, only I didn't know it till the moment I heard that line in the Joni Mitchell song. I wish when people ask me how I got sober I could come up with a formula that seems logical and would work for everyone. But the only answer I can come up with now is, I was ready. And life has been good these past two and a half years. So much has happened. Even if it's not at all what I thought would happen."

Burt explains. "The first year or so of sobriety was a revelation just for the physical changes. In fact, things got so much better so quickly that it was almost disturbing. For starters, I looked better. I started losing weight now that I wasn't full of alcoholic bloat. My eyes got clearer. I was just more alert, all around. I knew that what I saw in other people in meetings, a kind of visible physical well-being, was happening to me too. I even started working out with weights. I actually have a waistline, now, for the first time since I was about twenty. No more vomiting, no dry heaves. No more strange bruises that seem to come from nowhere. I started sleeping like a log—at least, eventually I did. The first six months I had my bouts with insomnia. But they melted away after a while. I quit smoking last year. I went through torture—it was worse than giving up drinking in terms of physical withdrawal—but with the help of what I was learning in the program, I did it, and I've stayed stopped. I got a job. I met a woman—and I got married eight months ago." Burt shakes his head. "You are looking at a changed man." He pauses again, no longer smiling. "And it's all great, right? I mean I should be feeling nothing but gratitude, shouldn't I?"

Burt's brow screws up into a frown. "That's the bitch of it. I know I should be grateful. And hell, I am—really, a lot of the time, I am. I've actually got a life instead of just a big alcoholic cloud of a dream world. But the dream—that's what rankles, still. My dream of being an artist. I feel like somebody threw a net over my talent and ran off with it. I just don't seem to have the stuff anymore. I can't get myself to do anything. You don't know how much I identified myself with that image of a genius artist; I mean, I was going to bowl the world over! And now . . . I'm ashamed, if you want to know the truth. Ashamed of the job I've got. Ashamed of the 'normal,' nice life I've got. I love my wife, and amazingly so much is easier than I thought it would be for us. I mean, I'm learning not to be a monster one day at a time. Not to be so selfish. I'm discovering so much about having a relationship; even sex is better now, although I went through some pretty strange changes about having sex without being zonked out of my mind. But I'm not—I'm not *wonderful*. And that's what I want to be. I want to be king of the hill. I want to be special. I want the heavens to open up and glorify me. I want to feel exalted. I don't want a nice life; I want a *terrific* life."

Burt describes his job sheepishly. "I'm the manager of this Italian restaurant. First I was a waiter, which was about all I could do when I was newly sober. I carted plates back and forth, grinning like a moron. But as I got more sober, my smarts came out a little, I guess. The guy promotes me, and here I am, a big wheel at Luigi's! I'm so embarrassed, when I get into a certain head about it anyway. But the real secret is"—Burt turns a little red—"I *like* it. Here I am, the great undiscovered artist, and I actually like ordering olive oil and making sure the tablecloths are clean and getting the flowers and paying vendors and checking the menus and dealing with customers. I actually take pride in all this. I like the guys I work with—it's a big Italian family. When I don't get into a funk about how I'm wasting my talents, I'm actually pretty satisfied. But then the old ego starts waking up, and I think, what the hell am I doing? All the years I spent doing art, all the dreams I poured into it. Yeah, I'm a drunk, but also I worked really hard at something that now I find I can't seem to do at all. It hurts."

Burt says that when, at his sponsor's suggestion, he did a Fourth Step on his work experiences, he realized that it took some effort to figure out what was a genuine desire to do art and what was an attempt to get acclaim and glory and attention. "Not that there's anything wrong with wanting that," Burt says. "But when I'm honest with myself, I can see that the main thing I lost about art when I got sober was the drunken fantasy, the genius role I could play when I was bombed out of my mind. Screwed up as that role may have been, I really cherished it. It was who I thought I had to be. But now that I'm sober—well, I can't play that role the same way. I still *want* to a lot of times— it's what I mean when I say I want the heavens to open up at how great I am, or that I want to be adored by everyone. But I'm not out of my mind enough to lose myself in that fantasy anymore. So all I've got is this ache, this nagging feeling that I'm not who I ought to be.

"The funny thing is, though, that when I accept who I am, and stop beating myself up for who I'm not, I sort of like the new picture. I like who I am at work. I'm a pretty decent guy. Reliable. Not so full of myself. I do my work when I say I will. I bring home a decent amount of money. Maybe there's something to be said for who I am now."

None of this is to suggest that Burt may not someday return to art. On the evidence of more recovering people than I can count, a life in sobriety can be every bit as externally wonderful as Burt wants his own life to be. Dreams can become reality. Indeed, it seems that in sobriety we learn for the first time how to allow our dreams to become reality. But we also learn to allow who we are to come out in whatever ways it has to.

"For now," Burt says, "I'm a damned good manager of an Italian restaurant. I don't think I'll be doing this forever. Who knows, once I've sorted out what I might really want to do in art from the old fantasies, maybe I'll find the 'stuff' again and return to it. My sponsor says he knows a lot of creative recovering people who've just needed time to regain their ability to create. What I'm going through now is humbling, but it's also a revelation. Maybe I can be a lot of different things than I thought I could. Maybe I'm okay even if I'm not a genius artist at the moment. It might be just fine to be the manager of Luigi's."

Burt is slightly more convinced now than he used to be that his art block isn't a reason to give up on anything. "You gotta be flexible," he says. "And patient. My sponsor tells me that nothing anyone does goes to waste. In fact, he came up with this parable about a sculptor, appropriately enough. It's a good one for me to remember when I want to give up, when the depression of getting through the tedious, boring shit I gotta do day after day threatens to overwhelm me—when the idea of a drink gets appealing again. He says to think of a sculptor, a guy who sweats for years to cut and haul a huge chunk of good marble out of a mountain. Then he spends another couple of years pushing and pulling and rolling the thing up the hill to his studio. Then he spends all his money on tools to carve it with. He's hungry, the landlord's at the door threatening to evict him, and suddenly he thinks, 'No, it's too much. I can't go on.' But it's at precisely that moment that he *has* to go on. All his hard work has been leading to this promise of completion. There's a sweetness, a satisfaction—an *importance* to the work remaining, even if it promises to be just as hard as the work that preceded it. You wanna root for the guy: 'Don't stop.' 'Landlords can be dealt with. You can find food. Don't let anyone deter you from what you've spent your life doing. A magnificent, abundant fruition is ahead.'

Everything in that sculptor's soul is right when it cries out, 'Don't stop now. Go on.'"

Burt smiles. "Hell, maybe I've got the stone halfway up the hill and I don't even know it! If there's one thing I've learned about being an alcoholic, it's how quick we are to judge the hell out of ourselves. Maybe I'll turn into an artist who gets his inspiration from lasagna! Who knows what this Luigi's business might be preparing me for? But the thing is, like my sponsor's parable says, don't decide you're through. Keep going. The miracle will come, even if it may come in some pretty unanticipated ways."

Patience: That may be the most exasperating word and concept to all of us who are recovering but aren't where we think we should be. Trust is another exasperating idea, especially when you're consumed with impatience for what Elizabeth called "my piece of the pie." But so many third-year recoverers show me by their example that miracles can take time to spin out. Burt's sculptor parable is a useful one: How do we know what we're in the process of creating, simply by doing "the next right thing"? We never know precisely what seeds we plant. And miracles grow from those seeds, even though the forms they take when they flower may astonish us, even though the rate at which they grow to fruition may not be the rate we'd have chosen for ourselves.

But perhaps that's good. Remember the "overnight success" of our Hollywood screenwriter Dennis, and his realization that if it had come one moment earlier than it did, he might well have taken a drink over it? It's just possible, Dennis tells us by his experience, that things may be coming to us at exactly the right rate and in exactly the form we need. "All I've really got to do is the next thing in front of my nose," Burt says. "Sure, it pisses me off when I find myself ordering cans of tomatoes instead of creating a Pieta. But who knows what those tomatoes might lead to? I spent so many years blowing my life to hell. Maybe this slowness is just what I need in order to heal."

At the best times, third-year recoverers tell me, you can find peace in surrendering to reality, in accepting who you are and what you're doing right now as somehow necessary and perfectly okay. At the worst times, when you feel like jumping out of your skin with impatience, you can remind yourself of something you've spent over two years learning: The feeling will pass.

A new sense of success and a new sense of time: these are two common dividends of sobriety as we go on. As we discover more and more about ourselves, new possibilities of who we might be begin to flower. It's part of the greatest adventure sobriety offers us: discovering who we are and what we have the capacity to become.

But we get stuck too. And much of what we get stuck in is our own behavior, which sometimes can feel just as unmanageable, restrictive, and frighteningly compulsive as the alcoholism or drug addiction we've turned to AA or NA to recover from. It might be sex or food or work or money. Escape hatches abound. Alcohol and drugs aren't the only ones many of us need to confront.

Let's meet a number of recovering people in their third year of sobriety who have found that now's the time to take a closer look at these issues.

two

Dealing with Other Addictive Behaviors

The term *addiction* has been so widely and indiscriminately applied that it sometimes seems to have been drained of meaning. Because of this, it might be a good idea to offer a working definition—not one that I've made up, but one that has emerged in the professional field of alcohol and drug counseling. According to Dr. Arnold Washton of the Washton Institute, an outpatient clinic in New York City to which every manner of addict has gone for counseling in recovery, a broad and sensible definition of addiction runs as follows: "If you've found it impossible to quit any behavior that is significantly impairing your life—whether in external ways or in the way you feel about yourself—you're a candidate for recovery." This is indeed a broad definition, but it makes one thing clear, something that isn't news to any recovering person in the third year of sobriety: An addictive behavior is something you can't quit even when you want to, even when you know it's messing up your life.

It's by no means true that all recovering alcoholics and drug addicts are addicted to other substances or behaviors than the ones they've surrendered to in AA or NA. It's clear to me that a number of recovering people experience a general lifting or easing of their desire to act addictively or compulsively in every area of their lives. The Twelve Steps as practiced by people in AA and NA can exert a pervasive magic, because program principles address and can help with every aspect of human motivation and behavior.

However, it's clear that many recovering people *do* have problems with behaviors or substances other than alcohol and drugs, problems that meet the criteria of the above definition of addiction: You can't stop doing it even when you want to. Sex. Food. Money. What does that random word-association test elicit from you? (Don't all groan at once. . . .)

A clear finding in the research I've done for this series is that for many recovering people, addictions tend to manifest like bumps in a rug. Push one down here, it pops up over there. As noted before, this isn't the case for everyone—some people do learn moderation and balance in all aspects of their lives, simply as a result of not drinking or drugging, going to meetings, and working the program. But from my observations, I have to speculate that the majority of us aren't this lucky.

Whatever the root of any addiction may be (and the jury is still decidedly out about how much is nature, how much nurture), part of it seems to be an urgent, underlying hunger, a profound feeling of *dis-ease.* Certainly the bedrock miracle for all of us is that we've managed, one day at a time, to stay away from alcohol and drugs; nothing can take away from that. But in most recovering people's experience, that searing hunger, the perception of a void inside that urgently needs filling and that used to keep us drinking or drugging, doesn't magically go away just because we've stopped drinking or drugging. Even those useful tools we learn in AA and NA—"working the program," assiduously "turning it over," doing more than one fearless moral inventory, acting "as if"—don't always keep us from grabbing for that next piece of cheesecake, racking up more debt with credit cards, seeking validation through yet another anonymous sexual encounter, or reaching for any number of other escape hatches.

These additional addictive behaviors can be incredibly disheartening. As one young woman with nearly three years in NA and AA puts it, "Now that I'm sober, how come I'm not cured? Why isn't *everything* better? And I know it's not just me. I hear about other people in meetings feeling addicted to lots of stuff, being torn apart by it. Why do so many of us, even in sobriety, still feel hooked to behaviors that we know are harming us but that we can't stop?" By the third year of sobriety, many of us can no longer ignore or "put on the shelf" our nagging worries and doubts about these kinds of behaviors. Some of us may already have done some digging into the territory, perhaps you've already attended meetings of Overeaters Anonymous, Codependents Anonymous, Sexual Compulsives Anonymous, or Debtors Anonymous. Perhaps you've gone into therapy to deal with these problems. We all bring to our third year a variety of approaches to these other addictions. But whatever we've done or not done, the evidence I've amassed makes it clear that by the third year we usually feel it's time to take a closer look at all this. The discomfort we feel is just getting too great.

Sex, love, food, money, work: Third-year recoverers are discovering much about these troublesome realms, with some surprising results. Perhaps the most general surprise is that we have more capacity to explore and learn about our "stuck" areas than we thought we did.

Let's take a look at some inroads third-year recoverers have made into this territory.

Sex and Love: The Hunger for Contact

For most of us, sex and love constitute a highly charged area. In no other emotional arena are societal and familial taboos more potent; nowhere else do human beings generally feel less adequate, more vulnerable, more on the defensive. Old messages we've internalized from society or family assail us. We're convinced that our sexual and romantic longings and fantasies are bad, irrational, or foolish. We mistrust our desires; we're not sure we're normal; we've got any number of doubts about our attractiveness, our capacity for intimacy, our lovableness or ability to love.

Few human beings escape problems in this area, but for recovering addicts and alcoholics the going can be particularly rough. For many of us our addictions were fueled by an intense desire to make contact, make life a party, or at least numb the pain of our loneliness. Some of us weren't able to conceive of having sex without getting wasted; then, when we discovered we were, after all, capable of having sex sober, sometimes we fell on the discovery like starving animals who couldn't get enough. The desperate desire to force some semblance of intimacy, to lose ourselves the way we used to lose ourselves when we got high, to get "validated" by arousing the sexual or romantic interest of somebody else makes this a powerful, mysterious, and often frightening realm.

Geraldine, who at forty-four has a little over two and a half years of sobriety in AA, finds herself particularly unnerved by the force of her romantic longings. "I come from an old Virginia family," she says, "a family with a long and proud history, back to the eighteenth century. Generations of women in this clan were brought up to espouse a strict code: We were ladies on the outside, as gracious and accommodating to 'our men' as we could be, but we ran things undercover. Sort of steel under velvet. Problem is, I never seemed to be able to develop the steel part."

Geraldine fell in love in high school with a renegade "greaser" and became pregnant in her senior year. She was shunted off to an aunt's house to have the baby, forced to drop out of school, and given a small income to leave the county and set up household where nobody knew her. "It really was like a Victorian novel. And yet I never thought they were being cruel; they were just doing what two hundred years of family policy had taught them to do." Geraldine had been a bright student in high school: "I was vying for valedictorian," she says, "when I got pregnant and dropped out of school. Colleges had already made noises about offering me scholarships. But now, suddenly, I was a mother, and cut loose from all that, all my dreams. I tried to love my baby daughter, but I was a terrible mother. I didn't know how to do anything. I was a child. I'd lose my temper at her when she wouldn't stop crying. There was no one for me to turn to. I was too proud to ask for help. I hate to think of the hell I put my baby through. I feel so guilty for it today."

Geraldine began to drink heavily during this time. "It was my only solace. I got a job working in the town library, which was wonderful because it got me near books, and I put myself on a college reading list, staying up all hours to read Plato, Thoreau, Chaucer, Milton, Wordsworth—God, it was wonderful! But I always had cheap sherry, bourbon, or brandy; literature and alcohol seemed the least I could do for myself in those days. I'd work, pay a babysitter to take care of Angie, my daughter. After work, I'd put Angie to bed, and then I'd read and drink. That was the pattern."

It was also the pattern to ignore Angie's frequent tantrums and crying. "After a while, I could just sort of mentally tune her out—which the liquor helped me to do. A huge rift grew between me and my daughter. It got worse when she grew up. She was quiet enough at home; after throwing a lot of tantrums as a baby she seemed to realize that wasn't working, so she learned to keep it all in. Until she got to school—then she'd throw screaming fits. I can't tell you how many meetings I had with her teachers, with the principal. She was put in special ed courses for difficult children." Geraldine's eyes start to brim. "It's so hard to talk about this," she says. "It's as if Angie never had a mother. I simply didn't care. I had my books and my brandy and that was it. I was a completely absent mother to my child."

At fourteen, Angie ran away from home. "I went through some halfhearted attempts to find her," Geraldine says. "She finally showed up at my mother's house; she refused to come home. My mother decided to keep her; she'd always known I was a 'bad seed,' as she put it, and she felt more compassion for my daughter than she ever had for me."

Geraldine was now drinking during the day as well as at night, and soon was fired from her job. "This was a sign," I thought. "Time to get the hell out of the south. Move to a big city—New York. Become a writer. Be someone artistic. Finally prove how special I really was." Geraldine's next ten years were a steady decline. "I never lost my southern girlishness," she said. "People would be amazed to meet me in all the rock bars and after-hours clubs I hung out in—I always seemed so innocent to everyone. What was a nice girl like me doing in a place like this? And I suppose I did nurture that helpless girl routine. Partly because it was true. I'd never grown up. From the moment I'd had my baby and started drinking, I sort of stopped growing. It didn't matter that I was in my twenties, my thirties, finally my forties. I was still a kid, a teenager."

Geraldine was, as she puts it, "handed from man to man. Almost literally. I fell in with a rock band when I first got to New York and slept with all the members. When they got it together to go on tour, I agreed to look after their rat-hole apartment along with the lead singer's brother, who then became my lover. Some months later he overdosed on heroin. Strange, I never did get into drugs like that, I guess because alcohol always did the trick for me, but maybe also because of that southern family 'ladylike' business—ladies would never do heroin! Anyway, he died. I went to the funeral with his best friend, also a junkie, who then moved in with me. And on it went."

When, almost three years ago, Geraldine ended up in a detox, she says, "It didn't happen because of any conscious choice. There was no man in my life. I didn't feel I had anywhere to go. I'd gotten so drunk that a bartender actually threw me out of a bar—something that had never happened before. I was half sitting, half lying down on the curb. A beat cop hauled me up, radioed for a car, and got me into a detox. I was glad to go. I wanted a bed to lie down and die in. That was it: I wanted some-place to *die.* That was my only aspiration."

However, detox "took." Geraldine was moved by a man who spoke at the first in-house AA meeting she had to attend; he re-sembled the man who had overdosed on heroin. A tiny bit of hope was illuminated for her. Maybe she was ready to change. She was so exhausted, so depleted. What else was there for her to do?

Now in her third year of recovery, Geraldine says that she feels humbled by the experience of sobriety. "It's incredible that I'm able to get through day after day of life without picking up. I've actually gotten back in touch with my family. My daughter is already a grown woman, and . . ." Geraldine can't prevent more tears from welling up. "It's so painful. She still hates me. And it's pretty obvious she's turned into a drug addict and drunk too. I have to give this time, I know that. I don't blame her for hating me. I can only hope that who I am now will somehow let her know that she can learn to trust me again."

While Geraldine says that she still often feels hobbled by ter-rible pain and regret, she is beginning to accept on a deeper level that she can't fix her daughter or force her to behave differently. She's been trying to focus instead on her own feelings and be-havior, which has led to a whole new area of difficulty. "It's these damned romantic fantasies," she says. "If only I could surrender to *them.*" Geraldine says she's guilty of doing the "thirteenth step"—the jargon her AA group uses for going to a meeting to meet romantic partners rather than solely to get sober. "I can't keep from falling in love all over the place. It's the same damned thing I did when I was drinking! Well, it's not exactly the same. I mean, my behavior is different. I've only actually gone to bed with someone twice in over two years, and that's an incredible change from the steady sexual encounters I had when I was drunk. But the energy I've expended on so many men, even if I didn't have a sexual relationship with them—it's tearing me apart. I'm so *hungry*. That's what it boils down to: My need for contact, for someone interesting to love me, for some imagined perfect union—it knocks me silly. I've actually missed work getting sick about this or that man not returning my call!"

It hasn't helped that the men Geraldine falls in love with are, as she describes them, "all wounded animals. It goes back to the first boy I was with, Angie's father. The old rebel without a cause. Sullen, hurt, withdrawn—and incredibly attractive. It's like I've got radar: If someone like that is anywhere within my range, look out, there I go."

Geraldine's romantic obsessions now strike her as addictive. "I started going to a few Sex and Love Addicts Anonymous meetings," she says. "At first I was a little put off. I mean, I don't have sex very much anymore. I couldn't identify with all the people who have anonymous sex; as much as I got into terrible relationships when I was drunk, I always knew who I was with. And I suppose I'm sort of proud that I'm *not* jumping into bed with just anyone. That's not my problem; it's what goes on in my head that's the problem. It's these damned romantic longings that keep me up nights. But I began to see that everyone in this Sex and Love Addicts group feels a similar hunger, even if they express it differently than I do. And it does help to hear them. It helps, I suppose, because it gives me some more compassion for the huge hunger that's at the center of me. I see other people, both women and men, who go through the same thing. It's like we're all searching for one perfect partner or environment that will take care of us forever, completely. One cure-all answer to everything. And we're realizing, finally, that there isn't such a thing. So we have to explore some alternatives."

Recently, Geraldine has seen that she might be able to apply what she's learned as a recovering alcoholic to her equally burning addiction of romantic obsession. "At first I just beat myself up for not being able to get over it. I'd forgotten all I'd learned about patience, and being kind to yourself, and turning it over, truly trusting that 'in God's time' things would work out. In my life as a recovering alcoholic I've seen so much get better when I learned to let myself be. The problem is how I keep judging myself. Why can't I just calm down and let my relationships and life just evolve? Why can't I be *normal?* And not want to throw myself off a bridge every time one more emotionally inaccessible man withdraws from me? I'm beginning to see it's precisely those 'why can't I's' I've been hurling at myself that are the problem. Sometimes you have to accept that you're stuck in order to get unstuck. And I've never truly done that before. And then I think, it was accepting that I was stuck in alcoholism that allowed me to recover from it. Maybe I do know what this means. Could the same thing work here?"

Letting up on yourself, being patient with longings that won't go away, and being compassionate about what has generally been a lifelong hunger for contact and a feeling of completion are all attitudes worth cultivating; they can help heal the raw wounds of romantic obsession. But sometimes your own self-loathing can get in the way so much that achieving this kind of self-compassion seems unthinkable. Witness Pedro.

At thirty-four, Pedro is a dark, lively man with captivating deep brown eyes. "Bedroom eyes," he says theatrically. "At least that's what most of my lovers tell me." He has always, by his own admission, been "the most cheerful guy in the world. I make friends easily. I mean, I'm pretty damned charming, you know? Maybe that sounds conceited. But all it really means is that I've learned to play a game pretty well. I know how to sell myself."

Selling himself is something Pedro literally used to do. "I was a hustler when I first hit San Francisco. I'd grown up in L.A.—a real lower-class barrio kind of thing. My father was Mexican, my mother Irish. What a combination, huh? I got out of that house as quickly as I could. Half the time they were drinking; half the time they were hitting each other. All the time they were yelling."

Pedro says that being a hustler in San Francisco wasn't so easy in the "gay capital of the world. I mean, it's not like I was the only cute gay kid in town. So I had to make sure I was special. It's like in that musical *Gypsy:* 'You gotta have a gimmick.' My gimmick was I'd do anything for a price. Which meant I got into some pretty strange scenes. Don't want to even think about some of them, much less mention them. But man, my real gimmick was, I always smiled. I always made the guy feel like he was special, like he was attractive, like he was worth something. Got a lot of repeat business. And I loved it, in a way. It was like I got the world to pay me to love me! Sounds like a pretty good deal, doesn't it?"

The deal got a little less good as Pedro grew older and was no longer the new boy in town. He got more wasted on drugs and booze, and was on what he says was a pretty inevitable downward spiral for "boys in the business. I mean, after a while, who wants to see the same tired old body, you know? The same world that was paying to love me was also using me up. But I'd always been pretty smart. For some reason, I always was attracted to intellectual types, guys who talked like they went to college, wore glasses, sounded classy. So I played innocent. Who me, a hustler? Never in my life. I'm just a poor kid trying to make it, looking for an understanding man. Got into a few 'relationships.' I'd move into some guy's apartment, set up housekeeping—and, one after another, I'd get bored outta my mind. I'd go back to the streets to see if I could attract some business, you know, hawk my ass again. I was hooked on that. Making someone crave me more than he craved anything in the world. I didn't want to be loved; I wanted to be worshipped. I couldn't get enough." Pedro's "peccadilloes" would get found out by whatever unsuspecting lover he happened to be with, and then "I'd be out on my ass again. The drugs and booze increased. Getting thrown out is pretty high drama, and I love high drama. Just gives me more reason to get wasted. Finally I hit thirty—retirement age for hustling. A year or so after that, I also hit bottom."

Pedro got beat up badly by "a drunken maniac john who refused to pay me after we had sex. He must have been drunk to want to go home with me; I was a mess myself. But he turned nasty, and he worked me over something fierce. I was half-conscious but somehow got myself to a hospital emergency room. Sitting there, a wrecked bag of bones, in such incredible pain—it wasn't just physical, it was like this terrible sick pain that went right into my soul—I just knew I'd had enough."

Pedro says his recovery began that day. "I took to NA and AA real easy. I don't know why, but I didn't doubt anything I heard. I guess I was just ready. But it also helped that there were lots of different kinds of people in the rooms. I'd always divided up the world into johns and hustlers—you know, usually white rich guys who could afford to pay exotic minority types like me for sex. But AA and NA taught me that there are so many people in the world, so many different people. And nobody looked down on me because I wasn't a WASP. Nobody cared about anything except how was my sobriety? I began to get the clue that maybe, just maybe, it was possible I might be acceptable without having to earn acceptance, to throw myself into somebody's bed, say, or perform in some other way to please him."

In the nearly three years since he's been going to meetings, Pedro has felt much of the relief we've already recounted in other people's recovery experiences. But one thing that hasn't gone away is "that urge to be adored. Man, that was a drug. And it still is. You know, I thought it would all go away once I stopped using and drinking. But it hasn't—shit, in some ways it's gotten worse. There are times I think I'll go out of my mind if I can't get somebody to tell me I'm the hottest thing he's ever seen. And so—well, I'm not hustling anymore. I'm not young enough for that. And I'm really not ready to put up with the kind of bullshit I used to put up with. I mean, sobriety has made me get a little more careful. Amazingly, I keep coming up negative on the HIV test—a miracle, given what I've gone through. I don't want to kill myself, or get myself into trouble. But it's hard, man. Because when I get that look from somebody, the look from a guy who I know I've 'hooked,' who thinks I'm hot, I lose control. I can't resist it. It's like this endless need for conquest. It's exhausting and it burns me out sometimes, because I've got a sponsor and I work the program and I don't drink or drug, so why am I still so hooked to anonymous sex? I've got a lover now, someone I really care about, and I don't want to hurt him. I also don't want to get kicked out like I used to get kicked out. I've pledged complete monogamy—and what a crock that's turned out to be, huh? I feel like a loathsome little worm. My lover doesn't know I was a hustler. He never knew the kind of perverted shit I used to get into. And I guess that's it: It's like nobody, not even in the program, really knows what a worthless piece of crap I really am. Yeah, I've told my sponsor a lot. But not everything. I still haven't done a Fourth Step—I keep putting it off. How could I let out what a shithead I really am? The worst part is, sometimes my sobriety just doesn't seem important anymore. I mean, who cares if I'm sober if I'm still so fucked up?"

The self-loathing many of us feel may have very different roots than Pedro's self-loathing, but few of us have trouble understanding the sense of darkness, of terrible secrecy he feels about what he fears is his true (loathsome) self. So many recovering people are grateful when they hear someone drum up the courage to talk about his own brand of "darkness." Seeing someone actually let the light in is a real triumph, and a message of hope. It lets us know that maybe we might be able to shed the same light on our own untellable secrets. In fact, it was listening to his sponsor talk about some of his secret past that led Pedro to a recent breakthrough about his own past.

"My sponsor told me something I could tell was real hard for him to admit. When he was still mainlining heroin, he thinks he might have killed a guy. He'd shot up this guy with a huge over-dose, watched him nod out, stole the guy's drugs, and then got the hell out of there. He's gone on for all these years not know-ing if the guy ever woke up or not." It wasn't the lurid detail of this that got to Pedro—"Hell, I've been through weirder shit than that"—it was the obvious pain and vulnerability he could see in his sponsor's face and hear in his voice as he talked about it. "My sponsor just seemed so—I don't know, *human*, I guess. I felt this funny feeling toward him—I guess it was love. Yeah, this kind of unconditional love. I wanted him to know that I cared about him, that he was doing just fine, that it was his honesty and his sobriety that were terrific today. And it was amazing—it was like this whole flood of unconditional love came out of me. It had nothing to do with sex; it just had to do with caring. And then I began to make a connection: Maybe that's what would happen if I let my secrets out to him. Maybe he wouldn't reject me like everyone else in my life always had when they found out about the 'real me.' Maybe my being honest wouldn't mean he'd stop caring about me—maybe it might even increase his caring, just like his honesty had with me."

I wish I could report that the new light Geraldine and Pedro have allowed to illuminate their love and sex obsessions had magi-cally cleared everything up. By learning to feel more compassion toward themselves and slowly gaining clarity about their feel-ings and behavior, both Geraldine and Pedro have let up on themselves; their pain is less and the prospect of their obsessions lifting more completely is at least conceivable. But there are no simple answers to something as deep-rooted, unconscious, and fearful as love and sex addiction. The third year of sobriety often seems to mark the beginning of dealing with these feeling and obsessions. Moving toward and exploring "solutions" can't be expected to happen overnight.

However, we can be guided by our own experience of recovery from alcoholism or drug addiction. As Mick, a man with just over two years of sobriety in AA, puts it, "I'm amazed at how wide-ranging the help I get from meetings really is. It's so much more than just dealing with alcohol. I've learned that Bill W. was plagued by a lot of the same sex and love problems I've got. But this just increases the compassion I feel for him—and for myself. It certainly doesn't take away one whit from the incredible work Bill W. did for us in AA. It just reminds me that he was a recovering drunk too; he was human. And he never stopped trying to understand his own behavior better and asking for help in improving it. That's a strong power of example for me. My own recovery from alcoholism is proof that there's never a reason to give up. The program can give me so much if I'll only just hang in, work, and wait for it."

In trying to address our problems with love and sex in sobriety, the recourses we may end up pursuing cover a wide range. There are many other Twelve Step programs that deal with a spectrum of addictions, including love and sex. Many of us go in to therapy and achieve wonderful results: Therapy plus AA or NA can be a very successful mix. Some of us don't feel the need to go outside AA or NA for help. We may discover, with the help of friends and sponsors, that we can tackle much more than alcohol and drugs with the Twelve Steps we've been working all along.

But the first stage in confronting all of this involves compassion. We need to take the judgment out of analyzing our fiercest hungers. We need to see that there is a hunger beneath our love and sex obsessions that requires love and understanding, not censoring and censure.

This is never more the case than when that hunger manifests literally. For many recovering people, food constitutes as highly charged an addictive arena as sex. Let's take a look at how a couple of third-year recoverers have begun to deal with their own obsessions about it, and the deeper hungers it can mask.

Hating Your Hunger:
Some Third-Year Food Dilemmas

Shirley is a slight, quick woman of thirty; she's the last person you'd suspect had a weight problem. In her third year of sobriety in NA—"I was a speed freak, mostly," she says—her route in sobriety hasn't been what she'd call smooth. "I don't really know how it is for alcoholics, but my suspicion about people like me, people who were hooked on drugs like cocaine and speed, is that we often have different kinds of stuff to deal with, at least at first. Maybe all I'm saying is that I didn't get totally wasted and lose everything. I had a high-powered job, and I still do, managing a chain of travel agencies. I've pretty much always had a fair amount of money, traveled all over the world, looked okay, had friends and a few lovers. What happened to me was almost entirely inner. It wasn't that cocaine and speed didn't make me jittery and erode my physical health—toward the end, I started looking like a ghost: pale, skin and bones, nervous as a cat. But what made me stop wasn't really that. It was this terrible nagging pain in the center of me, a pain that drugs just finally couldn't get rid of. I felt barren, empty. And I kept trying to fill that emptiness with proof that I was a 'success.' But as much success as I was able to acquire professionally, it was never enough. Nothing was ever enough. Just before I decided to stop drugs, I felt like a jet plane without a pilot going way too fast, like if I went any faster I'd spontaneously combust in the air. An empty jet plane speeding nowhere; that's how it felt. My depression became devastating, while, as I say, my outer life was in pretty good working order. Of course, I don't know how long I could have kept up appearances if I hadn't stopped when I did."

Shirley went through what she calls "wicked withdrawal. At first I went to an inpatient clinic, where I was put on some kind of antidepressant medication while I was weaned off drugs. I suppose physically it helped a little. But I was still taking something, and that just triggered my desire to take more. I knew I had to get off everything." Shirley started going to NA meetings and talked to other people who knew what she was going through. Ultimately she was able to get off all drugs, prescribed and nonprescribed. "Life is a very different bargain now," she says. "I've felt periods of calm I never knew I could feel. I've learned to let up on my constant drive to succeed at all costs—a little, anyway. The program has helped me in a lot of ways. I feel like I'm living in some kind of reality now, not the surreal, pumped-up mania I used to feel. And all of that's great. Except . . ." Shirley lets out a long sigh. "Except for this damned food thing."

Part of Shirley's quest for success had always been to stay as slim as she could. "It was really how I rationalized taking drugs: to keep weight off. I'd been a little overweight when I was about eleven or twelve—not much, but enough to show in pictures I still have from back then. Well, I say 'not much' now, but the truth is, I took those pictures out of the family album and hid them. I hated how I looked. And when I lost weight in high school—I'd already started on speed back then—I vowed I'd never gain it back. I was contemptuous of anyone who was the least bit overweight. It just seemed self-indulgent to me. And I was jealous of people who didn't seem to care so much whether they'd gained a few pounds. How dare they flaunt their fat in front of everybody! I thought they were all a bunch of slobs. I'd never be like them. *Never.*"

Then, in sobriety, Shirley found herself gaining a few pounds. "Now that I was no longer pumping up my metabolism with speed, I started to gain weight. It was terrifying. And it put me on a regimen that I've only recently begun to realize is crazy. I did three things in rapid succession: went on a crash diet, joined a gym, and started running. I scheduled on my daily calendar exactly what amounts of what food to eat when, and I didn't dare miss a day of running or working out on Nautilus machines. About three months ago I got the flu, which ought to have kept me home. But I dragged myself out with a temperature of 101 degrees and made myself go through my regimen. It was very early morning, and freezing. I actually collapsed on the track in the city park. I've never felt so sick. When I finally managed to get a cab back to my apartment, my roommate took one look at me and said she was going to take me to the hospital no matter what I said. I looked like death warmed over. They actually admitted me, and put me on intravenous because I was so dehydrated."

It was then, Shirley says, that she began to see how crazy she'd become. "My sponsor came to visit me in the hospital and just shook her head. 'What are you so afraid of?' she asked me. 'What are you running from?'" Shirley had what she felt was her second "surrender" at that moment. "The floodgates opened. I talked nonstop about how unattractive I felt, how it was only by the greatest vigilance that I could keep from turning into a fat slob, that I could make people like me. I suppose what I did was a Fifth Step on food with my sponsor. All the way back to those girlhood days when I was convinced I was fat and ugly and unlovable. How whenever I was hungry it felt like I was doing something wrong. 'How dare you be hungry!' That's what I've always told myself. 'You should be *above* hunger. Hunger is for lesser beings, people who can't control themselves.' I see now that I clung rabidly to drugs because it kept away my hunger, which to me was a terrible sign of weakness."

Shirley has started going to a therapist and attending a few Twelve Step meetings for anorexics. "Now," she says, "I've begun to feel a whole new awareness in this area. It is still painfully hard. But I'm slowly getting comfortable with the idea that maybe my hunger is perfectly fine. In fact, it might be something to cherish! If I heed it carefully and compassionately, it might teach me something about who I am, what I need. My hunger isn't something to run from, or try to block out the way I tried to block it out with drugs. It's something to try to satisfy." Shirley smiles, "What a total change of attitude that is! That I've been running away from something I really need to run *toward.*"

Of course, many recovering people wrestle with a problem opposite the one Shirley faces: eating too much rather than too little. Lisa, a forty-year-old woman with twenty-eight months' sobriety in AA, says she's cultivated a shy, self-effacing manner, "quite consciously. I'm so ashamed of being fat; I'll do anything to make sure nobody pays much attention to me." Lisa says she has always been overweight. "Food was a great solace to me," she says. "It's the old thing about it being a substitute for love. My parents got divorced when I was a baby, and I lived with my mother, who worked all day long. I almost never saw her when I was a child. My grandmother brought me up, and I practically lived in the kitchen. Actually she wasn't a particularly warm, loving person, but she never stopped cooking, and, probably to keep me quiet and out of trouble, she spent all day feeding me. Food was the only attention I ever got. As a result, I was a fat child, a fat teenager, and now I'm a fat woman. I've never been anything else. Except, of course, an alcoholic."

Lisa began drinking in college, she says, "to take away the loneliness. I had zero self-esteem, and people seemed to avoid me as if I were a black hole. It was made worse by the fact that I fell in love with my roommate. I'd always had crushes on my female teachers growing up, but I thought it was just a phase that would go away. But here I was, supposedly a grown woman, and I had to come to terms with the fact that I was a lesbian. I was in a small, conservative college; I couldn't tell anyone about my feelings. My fantasies just amounted to one more reason to hate myself. Not only was I fat, I was a sexual misfit too! God had really done a number on me, I thought. I was a freak, a monster. That's really what I felt about myself. Food wasn't helping enough to block out how terrible I felt, so I added alcohol. And that, at least, could numb me out."

When Lisa graduated from college she moved to a larger city. "By this time I knew my attraction to women wasn't going to go away. And while I never imagined I could actually have a relationship with anyone, I knew that there were women's groups I could sort of sit at the back of and maybe feel less lonely. Talk about self-pity! Mine was bottomless." Lisa did end up going to some gay women's support groups, and she was riveted by one woman who talked openly about recovering from alcoholism, and how much she was learning to love herself, how much it was helping her self-esteem. "That's when I thought of going to AA. Not because I wanted to get sober, especially. But because, I thought, maybe it would work as a kind of group therapy for how bad I felt about myself. If it meant giving up drinking too, well, I was willing to try." Lisa started going to a gay AA group, got a sponsor who required her to check in daily, and managed to stop drinking. "It was so strange," she says. "I felt, at first, I was just doing it as an experiment. I don't know that I ever really defined myself as 'alcoholic.' Alcohol always seemed to be something I turned to because I was so messed up inside. It was the symptom, not the problem. But slowly, when I treated alcohol as the problem, as the thing that had really made my life unmanageable, things started to get better. At first I was terrified to open my mouth in meetings. So my sponsor suggested I go to round-robin meetings, where they go around in a circle and everyone gets a chance to speak. Doing that every day has begun to make me less afraid. In fact, slowly, it's like I've found my voice. My sponsor says it's incredible how much I've blossomed these past two years. She says even the sound of my voice is freer, like something inside me is loosening up. I'm getting more courage, now, to say what I feel. I'm learning that nobody will jump down my throat."

But Lisa is still having problems with food. "I guess it's one of those things that just won't stay on the shelf any longer. What's really brought all this up for me is, I finally did a Fourth Step, and what was clear to me was how much I still hated myself.

Especially how much I hated my body. It was like my body and I were constantly at war. As I looked at all the stuff I'd written about food in my Fourth Step, I saw that I was on a wildly swinging emotional pendulum: Food was both comfort and curse. I couldn't bear to eat less, and I hated eating." Like Shirley, Lisa discovered how much she hated her own hunger—which was, she realized, a way of hating something very central in herself.

"Just talking about how I feel about this has helped," Lisa says. "And now I'm doing something more about it. I've joined Overeaters Anonymous. I'm a sucker for group therapy; I love taking every chance I can get to be with people, now that I'm starting to hate myself a little less, so I've also joined a group of women who meet to talk about their 'food issues.' That's been helping too. There's not a self-help book on the subject that I haven't read. But sometimes I still feel like the most awful failure. I still can't seem to lose weight. I'm still so hooked to that old comfort, that entrenched belief that if I gave up food I wouldn't have anything to rely on to cover up feelings. But at least I've got more awareness about this now, at least I'm talking about it. As long as I don't drink, as long as I manage to keep up a bit of clarity and self-acceptance—which sometimes amounts to accepting that I'm still stuck—I feel like I've got hope. And in the meantime, I'm listening to so many people who feel the way I do. People who have become my friends. I don't have to do any of this alone; maybe that's the greatest miracle. Even though I'm still fat, even though I'm still hung up on food, there are people in my life now who love me, understand me, and want the best for me. That's incredible. It's so much more than I ever dreamed could be possible for me."

Allowing Yourself to Be Human:
Progress not Perfection

As with sex and love, food obsessions or addictions are generally very deep rooted, and it's a triumph for most recovering people who have problems in this area simply to increase their awareness of it. One healing message that Lisa has heard from people in the rooms has to do with the Twelve Step slogan "Progress not perfection." A real bugbear for so many people in recovery is the idea that somehow there's a "right" way of accomplishing recovery, a kind of final and complete sure-cure key that everyone but you seems to be on the track of finding. By the third year, few of us are strangers to this kind of self-flagellation, to blaming ourselves for not being perfect, for not being able to get over all of our "character defects" immediately.

An equally formidable obstacle is the idea we've already begun to explore that feeling any kind of hunger means there's something wrong with you. What a terrible judgment this is! Assuming that our urge to feel "complete" or "filled-up" is pathological is a very damaging belief to hold about ourselves. It is an assumption that quite simply tells us we do not deserve to be happy.

When we associate any hunger we feel with disease or addiction, how can we help but feeling stymied? What real chance do we have of becoming "happy, joyous, and free" if we mistrust every desire for pleasure? A terrible booming inner voice (call it the superego, if you're psychologically minded) drowns out all else: "If I dare touch anything that makes me feel good, I'll get hooked! Give me an inch, I'll take a mile! If it feels good, I'll end up regretting it!" We become terrible taskmasters. We tell ourselves that pursuing any pleasures means being a self-indulgent hedonist. So many of us are secretly and half-consciously convinced that what we really deserve is punishment and deprivation, that we need to be "kept in line" at all costs.

And yet, as Francis, a twenty-six-year-old graduate student in his third year of sobriety in AA and NA, puts it, "an even deeper part of me tells me that this is terribly wrong. Call it my inner child if you want. But that baby inside me needs to be fed. He wants to be held and pampered and given all the pleasure in the world. And I can't believe it's wrong to feed that child, to give him everything he needs. If I'm honest, the only time I feel truly happy—and serene and sober—is when I feel like I'm satisfying my hungers, not running away from them. I'm sober when I feed that child, not when I starve him."

Francis has been battling what he calls his "addiction to plastic. For the longest time, whenever I felt the least bit of anxiety, I'd go out, start flashing my credit cards and buying things. My sponsor is a self-professed workaholic. He says he's afraid to give himself a day off: The prospect of empty time scares the hell out of him. My girlfriend, who's got about the same amount of time in recovery that I do, feels hooked on *not* spending money. She says she started feeling cheap when she got sober, remembering all the money she squandered when she drank and drugged. Now she feels that if she ever lets go of the money she has, she'll never get more. Another friend of mine is a compulsive collector: He's got every imaginable pair of salt and pepper shakers the world has ever produced. No flea market is safe from him."

Francis laughs, "I'm not making light of us nut cases. This stuff is a pain for all of us. But I can't tell you what a buoyant feeling it is to realize that I'm not alone with my addictive urges. And to see that there might be something common to many of us at the root of all these addictions. It seems to me to boil down to an intense fear of deprivation, that old thing most of us felt when we drank and drugged: If we don't cram as much as we can down our throats, if we don't hold on to everything, if we don't reach for more, more, more, it'll go away. We'll have nothing if we don't have everything." Francis shakes his head. "What an exhausting way to think you have to live."

Francis says he's been helped a lot by something someone said at a meeting he recently attended: "'Deal with your addictions in the order in which they'll kill you.' That helps me set up my priorities pretty clearly. I have to remind myself that I am a success—a complete, raging, fantastic, wonderful success—when I get through the day without drinking or drugging. All the rest of my obsessions and compulsions—and believe me, my 'plastic addiction' is only the tip of the iceberg—will somehow work out. I *trust* that, I believe it with all my heart. All I have to do is look at the miracle of my recovery in AA and NA to see that feeling good about myself, learning to love and satisfy my hungers instead of fearing and fleeing them—all of that gets more possible, day by day. There are always actions I can take to get a little more centered, a little more conscious of the causes and effects in my life. And when I take those actions, I drain away some of the fear, and the desire to act compulsively."

As the people in this book have said and demonstrated, none of this need be done alone. And perhaps that's the most healing realization of all. The help to which we have access is infinitely abundant. "Increasing contact with my Higher Power for some reason seems to be increasing the sense that I'm okay just as I am, even if I'm still besieged, sometimes, by pain and compulsive urges," Francis says. "I'm worthy even when I screw up. And just accepting that makes it a little easier to face the places where I'm still stuck. I'm not a monster because I'm not perfect."

Francis sums up with something he says his sponsor tries to remind both of them when they feel these temptations (Francis, the urge to hit the department store and his sponsor, the urge to work all night or throughout another weekend): "My sponsor suggests that maybe it would be a good idea if we didn't always react to our fear and discomfort as if it were a hot coal. Maybe it *won't* burn us if we touch it, if we allow ourselves to feel it for a while. In fact, the very discomfort we've had the reflex to flee for so long might even be able to act as a wonderful guide to what's going on inside us, if we'll only let it.

"Dealing with all this other addictive stuff now seems to be an organic process, at least when I let my own discomfort speak to me," Francis continues. "It can tell me what I'm really afraid of. Like I said, sometimes it's a fear of deprivation. Sometimes I just want to break through depression or loneliness or boredom. Sometimes I'm angry and resentful, and I want to go out and get rid of the feelings, blindly, like I used to when I drugged and drank. But I need to remember that I don't have to go out there blindly and flail away, like I used to. I can stay right where I am and ask for help. Allow myself to go a little deeper. And I have a model in my own life for how to do this: I can start by surrendering to who I am, just as I did with my alcoholism and drug addiction, and then give myself time to explore what I find. Above all, my sponsor says, don't judge yourself. Take a few careful, clear-eyed steps. But try to choose aliveness. Don't choose the deadness of the same old ruts, if you can help it. Choose to take care of yourself, whatever that ends up meaning to you."

Choosing aliveness.

Is there a better definition for sobriety?

thRee

Being Open, Setting Boundaries:
Third-Year Relationships

By the third year of sobriety, most of us have come to the healing realization that we're not alone. Not that there aren't moments when you may still *feel* alone; the effects of having felt "terminally unique" for so many years can linger pretty doggedly. As one third-year recoverer says, "My first reflex is always to isolate, to think that nobody could possibly understand me. But by now I've heard enough people in meetings who feel the way I do that I've got a lot of evidence sobriety isn't something I'm grappling with solo. And I admit, it's a big relief." You've probably heard AA and NA referred to as "we" programs. In fact, from the moment Bill W. met Dr. Bob, the indissoluble atom of Twelve Step recovery has always been two people: one addict helping another. It takes at least two to recover; one can't do it alone.

Accepting this "we-ness" has some profound reverberations in our lives, out of the rooms as well as in them. As we go on in sober life, we begin to see how we connect not only to other recovering alcoholics and addicts but to human beings generally. That may be a lovely thought in the abstract, but it can have some unnerving consequences when you get to specifics. By "human beings" we mean your mother, your lover, your boss, your best friend, the corner grocer.

The very word *relationship* pushes a red button in a lot of us. As Patricia, a sixty-year-old woman in Philadelphia with nearly three years in AA, puts it, "It's like a Rorschach test to me. I think 'relationship' and instantly I see two ex-husbands' faces melded in with the boy who took me to my prom forty-two years ago, mixed with the man I just broke up with, side by side with the man I can't stop thinking about now. My boundaries go to hell. I'm sixteen and sixty, vulnerable, scared, angry, resentful. It's like something out of that movie *Altered States:* I lose all perspective, everything melts into some kind of weird emotional, changing, surreal, and very charged mess. Sometimes all I want to do is run somewhere and hide."

Of course, relationships include more than the "very charged" lover kind. Again, "people" means everyone from your family to your friends to your co-workers to strangers you bump into in the street or in a Twelve Step meeting. By the third year, the commonly suggested restriction, "Don't get into a relationship in your first year," has long been lifted. We're now implicitly given permission to reach out in a variety of ways. In fact, as we've seen, reaching out has been crucial all along, even during that taboo period of the first year: Recovery *depends* upon connecting to other people. But as we begin to connect more widely in the world outside the rooms, we often get into what feels like completely uncharted territory. As Patricia puts it, "I've never been here sober before. Every new contact I have with anyone is one I've never experienced before sober. Even after more than two years of sobriety, I often feel like a baby in social situations. Learning about being a friend, trying to act responsibly toward people at work, reopening the channels with my father, who's got Alzheimer's and is in a nursing home, and with my grown children: all of this is very strange to do sober. But I'm drawn to do it anyway. Whatever path I'm on in recovery, it's not only a path to deeper self-discovery, it's a path to making more and more connections to the world outside myself. I can't seem to be a hermit in sobriety, at least not for long. The longer I stay away from a drink, the more I seem to need to connect with people."

By the third year of sobriety, we're commonly exploring a lot more about these connections than we could bring ourselves to do in our first and second years. Patricia again: "It was enough just to get through the day sober in my first year, and to begin to see what my feelings were all about in my second year. In a way it parallels the Steps. My sponsor tells me that the First, Second, and Third Steps have to do with going inside myself, accommodating myself in a kind of private way to recovery. But by the Fourth and Fifth Steps, and on to the Eighth, Ninth, and Tenth Steps, making amends and admitting I'm wrong when I am wrong, I have no choice but to make some pretty conscious and, God help me, often frightening connections outside myself. That's what I feel drawn to do now, much as it scares me. I want to live in the world as fully as I can; I don't want to hide anymore. But doing that means facing a lot of uncontrollable feelings, and uncontrollable people. It's a wild ride, sometimes. It's hard to navigate the 'real world,' especially when it means dealing with people who aren't in the program."

It seems the more time we spend recovering, the more sobriety becomes something we realize we have to take out on the road and into other people's lives. Doing this can have some unnerving but also quite wonderful consequences. Let's take a look at some preliminary voyages a number of third-year recoverers are taking into this outer world of relationships. We'll divide the territory into love, friendship, and work.

Friends and Lovers:
Third-Year Forays into Intimacy

William is a quiet man of thirty-five with nearly three years in AA. He says he's aware he tends to come across as a hayseed: "I grew up in a small town in Minnesota, and people in Seattle tell me I still seem like some kind of dazed kid from the country." William moved to Seattle from his rural Minnesota home about six years ago, and Seattle was the scene of both his "bottom" and the beginning of his sobriety. "It's also the place where I started to see my life not as something that just happens to me, like I was some passive doormat, but as something I actually might be able to direct a bit with choice. That's been the greatest revelation in my recovery, that I'm not just something blowing in the wind with no direction. Sure, 'shit happens,' like the saying goes, but there's some shit I don't have to put up with—and that I have some power to avoid." But, William says, "Seeing the power I've got in my life to make it better has been a long time coming. And I'm still not really there yet. I'm still attached to a lot of old stuff, stuff that tells me I'm a worthless bum and always will be."

William's feelings of worthlessness go further back in his life than the disasters he says have characterized his adulthood. But those adulthood disasters were typical, he says. "Basically they amounted to boozing myself into stupefaction, getting and losing a string of nowhere jobs, and a marriage that was abusive in some terrible ways. Karen and I clung together because we needed something to cling to. Both of us wanted to get out of Minnesota, but neither of us felt strong enough to do it on our own. So we kind of latched on to each other like life rafts. We drank our way west, nearly killed ourselves on the interstate in a pickup truck that died as we hit the Washington state border. We had some idea that we'd be Bohemian artists or something if we ever got to Seattle. Seattle still has the reputation of attracting people who want to get away from the dog-eat-dog world back East. But all we ended up doing, once we finally hitched our way here, was camping out near the waterfront, getting kicked out of furnished room after furnished room for nonpayment of rent, and drinking ourselves comatose every night. Karen blamed our lack of success on me. She really put me through the wringer about not being a provider or having any ambitions. Everything was always my fault. And I was ready to agree. I had about zero self-esteem. I knew I was a fuck-up. Karen's mission was just to remind me that's what I was, a job she carried out extremely well. She finally took off and went back to Minnesota. I hung out on the Seattle waterfront until I couldn't stand it anymore.

"I remember sitting on the pier with a bottle of rotgut wine. I wanted to pitch myself into the water. I can't even begin to describe that feeling of depression, or self-hatred, or just total despair. And I guess, now, I'm glad for every moment of that despair. Because what I ended up doing was pitching in the bottle instead of my body. I'd known for a long time I was alcoholic; I'd even gone to some AA meetings with Karen, mostly for the free coffee and cookies. But in that moment on the pier I hit bottom; I decided I didn't want to get any worse. I knew where the nearest AA clubhouse was, and I ended up passing out on a couch there. When I came to, people were around offering me coffee and helping me into a meeting. By the grace of God, I haven't had anything to drink since that time."

William says his story is pretty much that of a "garden variety drunk. Actually," he says, "sometimes I wish it were a little less stereotyped. I have to say that what bugs me about the Big Book is the repetition of, you know, 'my life was ruined by alcohol, then I saw the light, and now I'm a joyful recovering alcoholic!' I mean, that really *is* sort of what has happened to me, but it sounds awfully pat. Makes it all seem like a simplistic equation or something." William frowns slightly. "But of course, the outcome of giving up drinking is not all that simple. My recovery is something I wouldn't give up for anything or anybody, but it doesn't always feel joyful. Especially when it comes to dealing with people."

In sobriety, William says that he's become painfully aware of patterns in his relationships that he can't seem to break despite being more conscious of them. "My marriage was pretty much the model: get into a relationship with someone who wants to change me, who thinks I'm not enough as I am, and then beat myself up for not being who that person wants me to be. I know it comes from childhood. My dad is the vice-president of the bank in my hometown, looked up to by everybody, makes a lot of money. My mother is a really good musician and piano teacher, and she's made a real success of that too. People come from counties miles away to study with her because of her reputation. I've got two older brothers. Both are married, have families, nice homes, and jobs. And then," William sighs, "there was William. The old 'why can't you be more like your older brother' deal came double for me: I had *two* brothers to not be as good as. All I ever wanted to do was be in a rock band. In high school I got together with some guys and that's what we did. That was the best time in my life. I don't know how good we were, but we made a lot of noise and kids liked to dance to us. Can't explain what a trip it was to see people getting wild and crazy because of something I was doing. That was a trip, all right. But we broke up and I started drinking, and it's been downhill from there. Kind of depressing to feel you peaked when you were seventeen."

William says that now, going on three years in the program, he's learned to feel a little better about himself. "But every time I go out with a woman, I can't seem to help re-creating the old scenario: I play the 'raw material' that some woman thinks she has the power to mold, she finds out I won't budge, and we both agree that I'm a failure. It's exhausting. And it's not only with women. I gravitate to bosses who do that to me. Even my first sponsor was like that. But when the deadline arrives, you can't come up with the goods. It's boring, after a while. Sometimes, at least since I've had my current sponsor, who's been teaching me to keep a sense of humor about myself, it's even hilarious. It's incredible the lengths I'll go to prove to people I'm a fuck-up."

William says that he thinks fate put him together with his second sponsor. "My first sponsor was transferred out of Seattle

by the company he works for. I hate to say it, but I was sort of relieved. He was a real severe, no-nonsense, by-the-book guy. And
in a way it was good because he did make me pay attention to
the literature; he quoted chapter-and-verse from the Big Book,
and expected me to memorize it too. He had no patience with
psychologizing. AA, for him, was a simple proposition: You went
there to keep from drinking. He had an incredibly low tolerance
for what he called 'airhead psychological bullshit': If people
didn't discuss alcohol when they spoke in a meeting, he sus-
pected them of trying to turn the meeting into 'group therapy.'
You haven't heard disdain until you hear that man pronounce
those words," William laughed.

"But I felt like I kept failing him. I kept questioning some really basic stuff. What was anybody really talking about when
they said 'turn it over'? Why did we have to keep going to meetings our whole lives? I couldn't make it all the way through the
Big Book. It sounded like some old-fashioned 1940s movie script
a lot of the time. I kept asking why the Steps were in the order
they were, and if you really had to do all of them. Who said you
did, anyway?" William looks like a mischievous boy for a moment. "He *hated* my rebelliousness. He finally said, 'You wanna
go back to drinking? Go right ahead. You wanna stay stopped?
Work the program!' Finally our conversations descended into
him telling me 'don't drink and go to a meeting' to just about
anything I asked or said to him. Well, maybe I'm being unfair. I
was really needling him by the end. He was a good guy, really. It's
just that I kept reacting to him as if he were my father. I kept dar-
ing him, sort of, to call me a fuck-up. The old pattern again."

William got George, his current sponsor, by what he says
looked like default. He now thinks there may have been some
behind-the-scenes Higher Power manipulation. "As much as I
didn't really get along with my first sponsor, I did feel a hole in
my life when he was gone. So I signed up in an interim-sponsor
book we have in my home group and left it to fate who'd contact

me. This guy named George called me a few days later. He was amazing. Our first phone conversation began with me in the middle. It was like, the phone rang, I said 'Hello?' and I hear this guy's voice on the other end shouting, 'Damn it, get the hell out of there, Mack, can't you friggin' *just once* let me talk on the phone without getting into trouble?'" Mack, it turns out, was George's dog.

"That pretty much set the tone," William says, laughing. "George is the most preoccupied person I've ever met. Mind goes a mile a minute. But it's his incredible good nature that's made the real difference to me. You know, by reflex, I kept expecting him to get down on some aspect or another of how I wasn't doing the program right. Or I was sure he'd tell me, just like everybody else I'd ever known had always told me when I complained for the umpteenth time about my stupid minimum-wage job I had working as a waiter at a coffee shop, 'Why don't you try *doing* something about it?' I never realized, till I met George, how much I *expected* people to get frustrated with me, and eventually to leave me. George didn't do any of that. He just listened. And then went off, maybe, on some weird tangent or other about something he'd done in his own life. I couldn't always see how it related to what I was going through, but after a while it didn't matter. What mattered was he wasn't judging me. It was amazing to feel, for the first time in my life, that I could be who I was and not get blamed for it. It was like, by letting me go on and complain about my lousy life and how much I rebelled against the program, George was letting me listen to myself. I realized I'd never done that before. Everything I'd ever said before was calculated to get a certain (usually negative!) response from somebody else. I'd never really talked to myself about stuff. I was always trying to get a rise out of a lover or parent or boss or friend. But George wasn't taking the bait." William laughs again. "I'm not sure this was or is his conscious method. I mean, it may be that he's simply not paying attention to me sometimes! You know those old Burns and Allen shows? Sometimes George seems like the male version of Gracie."

But the experience of relating to someone without feeling judged has turned out to be a key that opened up a lot of new territory. "I find that, with George's example as a kind of model, I'm listening to other people differently. I'm really playing around with the idea that you can just listen without lashing out or withdrawing. Maybe you can just *be* with somebody. What a new idea! I'm not sure when or if I'll be able to apply this to the romantic part of my life. I mean, sex and romance and intimacy and all that other crap is still so charged for me. I just broke up with a woman who was just one more Karen: I exasperated the hell out of her and she left me flat. But I feel a little different about myself this time around. I'm not so quick to get angry at myself, to feel that awful self-hatred again. It's like, slowly, I'm allowing myself to see what the patterns of relationships in my life are, without reacting to them like they were a two-week-old pile of shit. In other words, I'm beginning to see the stuff that happens in my life as data, as something I can look at and learn from. What it amounts to is finding out who I am, how I operate. And, you know, as much as I think George is off in his own little world a lot of the time, he does listen to me. Because he said, after I talked about all this stuff, 'Hey, man, welcome to the Fourth Step! Sounds like you're ready for it.' And, who knows? Maybe I am. I'd always been so afraid before of really looking at my life— but now, all of the sudden, I'm not so scared. Something seems to be changing in the center of me. Feels like a tiny bit of freedom that wants to grow bigger."

The data that our own lives continually offer us are staggering, as many of us come to see in the third year of sobriety. As William puts it, "I'm beginning to feel that nothing I do in my life doesn't reveal who I am. Even when I think I'm hiding and trying not to be myself, I'm still naked. My very defenses are part of who I am, who I've thought I had to be. The trick is to get a little distance from the noise and steam of daily life to see what it's all telling me."

Anna, a forty-two-year-old woman who lives in a middle class suburb of Boston, has had her own experience coming to terms with the "data" of her two and a half years of sober life, and how that data relate to relationships. Anna has been married for seven years to a man she's lived with for eleven. "It has been, to put it very mildly, rocky," Anna says wryly. "You know how in *The Scarlet Letter* Hester Prynne gets branded with the letter *A*? Well, believe it or not, I've actually got a birthmark on my shoulder in the shape of a *V*. *V* as in victim. It's only been in sobriety that I've begun to see how much complicity I've had in living up to that *V*. What I'm trying to do now, maybe, is have it mean Victory. But, God help me, it ain't easy."

Anna's husband is an on-again/off-again crack addict and alcoholic. "Sometimes he'll go to meetings with me and act like he's 'gotten it,'" Anna says. "In fact, he'll start lecturing *me* about how I ought to be doing in the program. But then he'll go back out—usually, lately, to crack. And our lives will turn back into a nightmare. Rationally, I know I don't have to put up with this. I mean, I go to Al-Anon meetings. I've got a therapist and a sponsor. My sponsor has just gotten to the point where she's dead silent when I go on about what an asshole Jack, my husband, was the night before. She's already told me that I don't have to put up with it, that I could just leave him. But she knows it doesn't help to tell me that. She knows I have to feel it for myself."

So why can't Anna make a change if her life with Jack is so miserable? "Jeez," exhales Anna as she considers the question for the millionth time. "If only it were a matter of logic. Again, I could give you a brilliant treatise on the psychological reasons for all this. Alcoholic father who left home when I was twelve. Distant mother who wasn't home much either because she had to work to support us. I'm the oldest sibling, so I turn into a mommy and bring up my four younger brothers and sisters. I'm the one who shoulders all the responsibility; that's my role. And I think I've got to do it because if I don't, nobody would stay around. Call it one big fat fear of abandonment."

Anna says the fear that she would never be able to hook up with another man is so overwhelming that she can hardly give it voice. "Jack goes on about how I keep gaining weight, how he's losing interest in me because I'm not the svelte young thing I was ten years ago, and it feeds how bad I feel about myself. I've been off drugs and alcohol for over two years, and that's been great. I mean, I'm showing up for my job. I'm a dental assistant, and a good one. I get a lot of help from the program and going to meetings. But something in the center of me hasn't budged, some great fear that I can't make it in the world on my own. Even if the man I'm with is bad for me, he's the only man I've got and the only one I'm likely ever to have. That's what that inner voice keeps telling me. And God, he cheats on me, keeps going back to this lover he had before he met me. Sometimes he tempts me with crack or booze when he goes back out again. He's just awful. But for the twenty-three hours that he's awful, there'll come one hour when he'll say something like, 'What would I ever do without you? I love you so much,' and I'm a goner again."

Like William, however, Anna has recently begun to see her life a bit more clearly as data, data that might be telling her something different from what she'd been able to see before. "I've always thought that the only relationship that mattered to me—in fact, the only thing in my life that really mattered to me, maybe more than my sobriety—was what I have with Jack. But recently something happened to jolt this. A friend of mine in NA, Becky, suddenly moved out of town. Becky wasn't my sponsor or anything; she was just a woman I'd grown comfortable talking with over the past two years. Her mother died, and Becky inherited her mother's house. She'd gotten a divorce a few months before, didn't have any kids, and, I guess, really felt like she wanted to start a new life. She shared at her last meeting that, now that her one remaining parent was no longer around, she finally felt freed to do what she wanted, to start a whole new life. I thought this was great. But I wasn't prepared for how I felt after she was no longer around to talk to. I couldn't believe how much I missed her!"

Anna says that Becky's sudden absence taught her that she really had no friends. "Becky had come the closest to someone I liked being around, having coffee with after a meeting, laughing with, just talking with about day-to-day stuff. I realized there wasn't anyone else in my life like her. And then—I knew it was irrational, but the feeling was so strong—I felt I'd done something to drive her away. That if her life here hadn't been so terrible, she'd have stayed. And obviously I wasn't enough to keep her here; probably, in fact, she was glad to get away from me. I projected all sorts of terrible stuff. But the main thing I was left with was this awful feeling of loneliness. I have a sponsor whom I call a couple of times a week to sort of 'report in.' But I realize all I ever talk to my sponsor about is how awful Jack is. And it's pretty much the same thing with my therapist. I didn't have any friends just to *be* with."

Anna says she's gotten over some of the pain of this now that she realizes "maybe I have a choice. Maybe I could look at the people I see at NA meetings differently. Maybe I could reach out a bit more, be more friendly. I guess the biggest revelation is that I've got more relationships in my life than the one with Jack. And maybe they could all be important. After all, when I think about why I've been able to recover from cocaine and Valium and all the rest of the stuff I used to take, hasn't it been, like the program says, because I'm hooking up with other recovering addicts? Those relationships are keeping me alive! I just never acknowledged that before. Maybe the world of people is wider and richer and more potentially nurturing than I'd been able to see."

As Anna begins to reach out to more people in friendship, one very welcome dividend is that she's finally accepting the Al-Anon "Keep the focus on yourself" message on a gut level. "Now that I'm getting some of my emotional needs met by my friends in the program, and allowing myself to value my friendships as important, I see Jack differently. Maybe he's not the be-all and end-all of my life. I'm still not ready to think of leaving him, but I *am* able to see our marriage a little more dispassionately. I just feel a little more open to what the world might be able to give me. Maybe it's a bigger, more interesting, and more abundant place than I'd ever dared believe it was."

While learning that you're not alone is, as we said at the outset, a crucial part of getting and staying sober, people I've talked to in their third year of recovery often experience their aloneness, and subsequently their connectedness, on deeper and deeper levels. An inevitable process of self-discovery seems to be set in motion by the decision to stop drinking and drugging, and to reach out for help to stay stopped. Commonly, as we go deeper into ourselves, we find new levels of fear and doubt about the possibility of being helped and heard and accepted and loved. And, eventually, we find that the program is strong enough to take us through those fears and doubts. Anna says, "I feel now like I sort of 'pop through' fear—I confront it, then surrender to it, and then something propels me forward and I'm out of it. I don't feel like I've got to cling as much as I used to. I'm beginning to think that something is there that will break my fall. Maybe I actually *am* getting taken care of."

Feeling as if you're actually being taken care of is something most of us yearn for. From many accounts of third-year recoverers (or from people at any point in their recovery), it's clear that few of us enjoyed that safe feeling of being cared for where we might expect to have found it: in our families. The unconscious attachments and fears and resentments that accompany our love relationships sometimes seem to quadruple when we take a look at how we feel about and react to our families in recovery. Progress here is, commonly, pretty slow. But it is possible. Witness Martha and her mother.

How Monkeys Get Caught, and Other Revelations About Family

"Not long ago I saw this National Geographic nature program about how they catch monkeys in Africa," says Martha, a fifty-five-year-old newly retired schoolteacher who is two months short of three years in AA. "What they do is dig a hole and put some brightly colored nuts in it. Then they wait for a monkey to come by and reach into the hole to grab the nuts. But the hole is only large enough to let the monkey's empty hand in; once he's grabbed the nuts, his hand is too big to pull out." Martha shakes her head with exasperation. "Now," she continues, "all the monkey has to do to escape is drop the nuts. His hand could slip out, and he could get away. But apparently no monkey ever lets go of the nuts. Each one struggles there, arm-in-hole, until the trapper whisks him away."

"Story of my life," Martha grumbles. Her ironic smile fades. "It's what I've been doing with the memory of my mother. It's finally dawned on me that a parent doesn't have to be alive to rule your life. When my mother died two years ago, it's like I reached after her, and got stuck. In fact, I feel like she's kept me trapped there ever since."

Martha says here mother was a gospel singer. "She made the rafters ring in our hometown church. She was a star. We were dirt poor, my father was a no-good drunk, I barely had a dress on my back, almost no food to eat, but Mama sang. And I must admit, when I was a little girl in church, I was so proud of my mother that I didn't care that our life was hell when we got out of church. Mama's voice was so beautiful and strong and stirring—everybody oohed and aahed at it. Didn't put any bread on the table, but they loved her voice. And she loved the acclaim. In fact, that was the problem. I never seemed to be able to give her as much love as she got from the full congregation. She hated her life. She wanted to sing, she wanted to be the next Mahalia Jackson, she wanted to go on the stage. The dreams she had! But we were stuck where we were, in a tiny rural backwater Louisiana nowhere town, and when she got at all realistic about it, she knew her dreams were in vain.

"I don't want to go on and give you a big psychoanalysis of why I never felt like I could get through to my mother. It's sufficient to repeat that she wanted a cheering audience, not a skinny, unmusical little girl in pigtails. I could barely carry a tune; I inherited none of her talent. I was my daddy's girl, appropriately enough since he was a drunk. Though God knows I wished I'd been my mama's. Daddy was a skinny, no-good, cheating wino. Quiet enough, didn't hit anybody, but useless. Instead of Mama's musical talent, I got his flat feet and propensity to drink." Martha chuckles a bit. "I've never understood people going on and on about what a great institution the nuclear family is! Almost everyone I hear in meetings today hated their childhoods! God knows, I hated mine. For starters there was my brother, who did inherit my mama's musical talent. He sang in the choir as a little kid and the preacher's wife taught him some piano, so that he was picking out tunes, playing Mozart and ragtime by the time he was twelve. Mama adored him. I hated him. He used to tease me unmercifully for being ugly, skinny, and tone-deaf. I railed away at a God that could give so much to my brother and so little to me."

Martha was good at school and hoped in vain to gain her mother's attention through academic prowess. "But no, it was always Johnny, my brother, it was always how wonderful he was, and how lacking in talent and ability I was. My daddy would sit in the kitchen drinking, and, sometimes, before he'd pass out, he'd pat me on the head, as if to tell me he knew what it was like to be an also-ran. I hated him for that—for giving in, for thinking I was the same kind of failure he was. And finally, because I couldn't get my mother to pay attention to me, I started to hate her too. I decided I'd do anything to get away from that family and that backwater town. I graduated from high school and got a scholarship at a big university in another state. So, physically, I got away. But emotionally I was still back home. In fact, I've been emotionally stuck back there for thirty-five years, even though I never once crossed back over the Louisiana border, except to go to my mother's funeral two years ago."

Returning for her mother's funeral brought things to an excruciating head for Martha. "For one thing, I was sober for the first time in my adult life, and I was scared out of my mind. It was still very early sobriety, and, frankly, I didn't know if I could keep from drinking. My daddy is still alive—amazingly, given the amount he's drunk all his life—and I knew the wake would be a flood of alcohol. My brother was there; I hadn't said a word to him in all these years. I was the renegade, the black sheep, the child who had abandoned her roots. Nobody much wanted me to come back, nobody much cared. It was rough. But I knew that I had to go. I couldn't let my mother go into the ground without— I don't know, I suppose it meant saying good-bye. Or maybe it meant trying to get a handle on what I felt, now that I was supposedly grown up and sober and my mother was finally gone. All I know is that it was a horrible experience. I was all but ignored. Somehow I managed not to drink. I came back up north as quickly as I could after the wake. But, like I said, I didn't bring all of myself back. Because part of me had never left to begin with."

The only member of her family Martha had seen throughout the past thirty years was her mother. "She came up to Atlanta to visit a cousin who extended an invitation and paid the fare every year for her birthday. Mama had once saved this cousin's little boy from drowning, pulling him out of a pond he'd fallen into, many years before. These yearly all-expense paid visits were the cousin's means of paying her back. But they didn't spend much time with each other. It was my mother's big annual trip, and she wasn't going to spend it chatting with an elderly cousin about the weather. No, she'd play the grande dame, demanding to be taken out to restaurants and to anything musical, like a jazz club or a piano bar, like she lived that kind of life all the time. It was her time to play the star, which she so yearned to do. I was acceptable at this time because I was educated and knew my way around cities. So I was a sort of chauffeur and yes-woman. She was such an embarrassing lady! God, how I hated those outings. It was a chore to take care of her, to see her in her one 'city outfit,' a great spangled, cheap, red and black tent of a dress. She always wore too much makeup in the city—after all, wasn't that how stars in the big city were supposed to look? As my drinking got worse, our main destination was a certain piano bar, where I knew I could at least get my nightly quota of booze no matter what kind of fool Mama made of herself. Mama never did drink much, but she sure as hell got up to sing. Unfortunately, as she got older, her voice got rougher, and people quickly got tired of her hogging the mike. Her 'city' songs were Bessie Smith blues-type stuff—nice in small doses, but overbearing when there's no letup. And with Mama, heaven knows, there was *never* any letup. I'd sit there drinking while she dominated the proceedings until she was politely but firmly asked to please sit down. I'd squirm in my seat, hating her and hating myself. Seeing Mama was torture. But I had to do it. I'm not sure why, but I had to."

Martha said her life had narrowed down to three things for the last twenty years of her drinking: "Teaching, bourbon, and passing out. I'd been married only briefly to a man I met in college. It lasted for about six months. We'd gotten drunk at his fraternity, and we got married because we wanted to go to bed with each other. Imagine having such scruples today! But back then, in my conservative youth, you didn't go to bed with someone if you weren't married, not if you were 'nice.' Well, marriage wasn't nice for either of us. We both were glad to break up. I found a job as an elementary school teacher and rented a small apartment in a suburb of Atlanta. And I drank. I had some friends from college for a while, but they all got married, moved away, started their lives. I just got drunk. Amazingly, it never kept me from teaching. That was like my badge of normality and competence. What little self-esteem I had went into my job. I suppose I became that proverbial school marm who 'drinks a little.' Anyway, my life got littler and littler until, when I retired, which I had to do because of a school budget cut, I found that without my job I had no life at all. I actually became suicidal. Certainly depressed enough to try AA, which I'd heard about because it was where my hometown preacher always told my mother that my father should go: 'Get him to AA!' He never went, of course. But at least I'd heard the acronym. And something in me, I still don't know what, but I'm prepared to call it a Higher Power for want of a better term, allowed me to reach out for help."

Two years ago, with her mother's death and her newly found sobriety, Martha found herself deeply rocked. "It was wonderful to stop drinking, don't get me wrong. A life without hangovers, without that constant, terrible grayness, how could that not be better? And I go to meetings every day. It gives my life some form, for one thing, now that I no longer work. But over the past nearly three years, I feel like a kind of huge roller coaster has emerged in front of me, taking me full speed ahead, with huge highs and then shuddering dips. What I'm really saying is, *feelings* have to do with memories, most of them memories of family, of how much I hated my mother toward the end—all of this terrible pent-up venom is gushing out. Sometimes I don't sleep nights, I obsess so about my family, how much they held me back, how little love I got from them, how much love from them I yearned for.

"My mother's death made me realize that I needed so badly to come to peace with my past. You know, one of the 'promises' in the Big Book runs, 'We will not regret the past nor wish to shut the door on it.' God, how I wish that were the case for me! But, you know, it just might be coming true—at least it might be starting to." Martha says that the other day she got out an old Bessie Smith album she hadn't listened to for twenty years; it had a lot of songs her mother sang in her last appearances at the piano bar. "I don't know why I wanted to be reminded of those embarrassing times, " Martha said. "But something in me told me to put the record on. And when I did, and heard Bessie sing, I had the most incredible vision. I saw my mother, in all of her loud glory—that tatty red and black dress, overwhelming all the crowd, barging in on neighboring tables, batting her overly mas- caraed eyelashes—and this flood of loving her came over me. What a courageous and pained woman she was! It was so clear to me that she'd had an ache in her own heart for love and recogni- tion that she never felt was filled. I felt for her in a whole new way. It's like the whole notion of *blaming* her lifted; it just wasn't especially helpful or illuminating to point the finger at her. All I could see was her own pain. And I felt his flood of compassion and forgiveness."

When Martha took the record off, the feeling stayed with her. "And it spilled over to my daddy and to Johnny, my brother. My God, I thought, here I go to an AA meeting every day and feel compassion for all these strangers, and I couldn't bring myself to feel the same thing for my family—at least not until now. I just had the strongest sense, a kind of spiritual sense, that we were all doing the best we could. And who was I to sit in judgment of any- body? It's funny, I'd never been able to do an Eighth Step, making a list of people I'd harmed and becoming willing to make amends to them. It terrified and sickened me to think of getting in touch that way with my family. But now I *wanted* to write that list. Because I saw that we all were due for a cleansing. We all were due for some clarity and honesty and compassion. I guess I was just ready to feel these things; it certainly didn't come as the result of willpower. I had tried before to *make* myself love and forgive my family, and I couldn't. But now, suddenly, with Bessie Smith's help, I could. And since that time, my whole life has felt lighter. Not that I'm not capable of resentments, or of getting angry over what I wasn't given as a child. I still can feel those things. But there's more space between me and my memories, more understanding and less across-the-board judgment. Of course, I still haven't actually contacted my brother and my father and done a Ninth Step. We'll see how all this works out in real life. But in my heart, I've come to a new readiness. And when I think of my mother now, I don't remember a self-absorbed, overbearing, and uncaring lady. I remember a woman in pain, and a beautiful voice."

As Martha said, the ability to shift her perspective about her mother was not the result of willpower. She wasn't seeing things differently and more compassionately because she knew she "ought" to. We've been seeing all along in this book something you've undoubtedly seen in your own progress through recovery: insights *ripen.* They won't come on cue or because we want them to. And we can't, with any profit, pretend to insights we don't really feel. "I used to give lip service to how important it was to be forgiving and compassionate," Martha says. "But actually feeling those things in my heart was a completely different story. Something had to develop in me before those feelings could really emerge. Sobriety has its own timetable, that's for sure. Patterns you've clung to for a lifetime don't go away overnight. But what an encouragement and a relief that they *do* sometimes change, sometimes of their own accord! I didn't know that Bessie Smith album would have the effect it did. Some readiness in me had matured without my having to will it into being. It's a whole different way of looking at your life, letting things evolve like this. And it's so much more wonderful than trying to force yourself to feel what you're not ready to feel."

Bosses Aren't Parents
(and Other Sober Surprises at Work)

The process of becoming aware of patterns in your life and your relationships is, on the evidence of third-year recoverers, strange and unpredictable. Stan gives quick examples of how it can work itself out in the job arena. "It wasn't news to me that I'd reacted to my boss as if she were my mother," says Stan, a twenty-eight-year-old advertising copywriter who has been sober in NA and AA for twenty-five months. "I mean, I'd known from the time she hired me that that was the dynamic between us. My boss, Harriet, was estranged from her own son, and I know she sort of saw me as a stand-in, as the son she wanted her own son to be. She was the perfect enabler, a dream boss for an addict. I'd come up with a fairly good morning's work, and she'd go on about how much talent I had, she'd call her friends and tell them about me—she'd really give me this sort of awful, embarrassing buildup. Then I'd go out to lunch, which when I drank and drugged meant several vodka martinis and two quick joints in the far end of the parking lot, and pretty much be useless all the rest of the day. She'd make excuses for me when I wouldn't return calls or come up with stuff on deadline. I was so creative, so *tortured* in a kind of artistic way. But she also resented me when I didn't come through—which was pretty much every afternoon, since I came back so wasted—but not like a boss, who would have just confronted me about screwing up and maybe eventually fired me. She'd act real concerned. Like, was I eating well? Was anything bothering me? Did I want to talk about it? And then, as if to encourage me to tell her equally intimate stuff about myself, she'd tell me totally inappropriate things about her own life. About the man she was seeing but who only wanted to go to bed with her, and she wasn't sure she liked him enough. She'd even tell me about her gynecological problems. The dynamic between us wasn't just mother and son. She was flirtatious too. And it was all fine with me, as long as I could keep drinking and drugging and getting paid." Stan squirms in his seat. "I don't mean to make her sound like a fool. She was a very talented and competent advertising executive, and a good person with a good heart. The mother/son and flirtatious stuff wasn't conscious; I know that. But those dynamics were still there, and there's no getting away from the fact that they were very screwed up. And when I got sober over two years ago, it was a huge shock to both of us. Because it quickly became apparent that the old patterns couldn't work anymore. The problem was, she wanted them to continue, and I wanted to get the hell out. God, it was awful."

The hardest thing, Stan says, was controlling his own temper. "Now that I was sober, it was so much clearer that my boss was treating me inappropriately, much too personally. I resented the hell out of her for barging into my personal life, asking me about who I was dating, my health, that kind of stuff. Before I'd just shrugged it off—or, who knows, maybe I was comforted by it in some weird way. It meant that she cared about me enough that I wouldn't get fired, for one thing. But I guess I was also more willing to be her son than I became later on. Later on, it was exactly like me rebelling against a parent. I was terrified of leaving. The advertising job market was very weak, and I was still so new in sobriety that I couldn't imagine having the fortitude to make a big change. So I took out my frustrations on my poor boss, just like I might have on a parent. In some ways, my work got better, just by virtue of the fact that I was conscious in the afternoons! But I'd snipe at her, really lose my temper. Once it was particularly awful. She'd discussed an account with one of our clients, telling him the opposite of what I'd said. When the client called to query me about the inconsistency, I just lost it. I stormed into her office and screamed at her, how *dare* she undermine the work I'd done for this client, who did she think she was, the whole bit. God, I was an asshole. And she was shocked down to her feet. She even trembled. But she was also really angry. 'I don't deserve your talking to me like this! How dare *you!*' she said. I half expected her to add, 'after all I've done for you,' like my mother would have. But she didn't; in fact, she became appropriately angry for a change. And that was a turning point for me. Because I realized down to the heart and soul of me that she and I had never really treated each other with the kind of respect and courteous distance I now knew I wanted in any professional association. We'd gotten into some half-conscious muck of friendship and work, neediness and insecurity. It was a mess. I knew at that moment that I had to change jobs, that I was really unhappy, not only with the working relationship I had with her, but with the fact that I wanted to advance in my career. And I knew that as long as I was with Harriet, that could never happen. Our dynamics were just too entrenched; she'd never willingly let me go. At least that's how it felt then."

Stan says the hardest thing he's ever had to do was quit that job. But it was also the most wonderfully relieving and illuminating rite of passage he's had in sobriety. "For one thing, Harriet did not dissolve into a puddle when I told her I was leaving. It turns out that more than a little of this mother/son dynamic had been coming from *me*; she wasn't quite so unprofessional after all. She even understood that I wanted to see if I could get a better position—and she encouraged me, giving me some names to contact, with the promise of a rave recommendation. I won't say it was all that easy for her—I'm sure she did feel in some sense betrayed—but, you know, AA and NA counsel us to see what our parts in situations are, and it was crystal clear to me that it takes two to 'enable.' I was as much a part of the sick relationship we'd had as she was. But now, in sobriety, I discovered I had the power to disengage." Stan takes the kind of deep breath now he says he did when he first felt the full relief of this. "I could actually take a responsible action! We came to a reasonable agreement—I would stay until she found a replacement for me and while I sent out my resume—and we got through it. There wasn't nearly the *Sturm und Drang* I expected. It was all so—sober!"

What we've seen so far are a number of third-year recovering people who have come to appreciate that they're not as entrenched as they thought they were. "I think we've got so many more options than we realize we have," Stan says. "When I drummed up the courage to leave my job, it was as if I'd pushed that big boulder out of my life—a boulder on which was carved 'Either/Or.' I'd lived my whole life, even in sobriety, convinced that things had to be one specific way or another. That was it. There was no other way: yes or no, black or white. But there are *loads* of other ways, maybe an infinite variety of ways things can turn out! As a recovering addict, I'm like every other recovering addict I hear talk in meetings. I'm terrified of change. But change is how things get better. So I'm terrified of something I really ought to embrace!"

Recovering people show and tell me that the relationships we have with other people reflect the relationship we feel with ourselves. Like Jacqueline, we find that what we feel inside tends to manifest quickly on the outside. This doesn't only mean that we tend to look good when we feel good (or not so good when we feel bad); we also gravitate to people who tend to corroborate the views we hold of ourselves. This is a stunning truth to most of us in recovery: the degree to which our outer lives reflect our inner ones. And the idea that we might actually, as William said, have a *choice*—that, as he put it, life isn't "something that just happens to me, like I was some passive doormat, but something I actually might be able to direct a bit with choice"—is probably the most heartening thing we can learn in sobriety.

"So many of us just repeat the 'Serenity Prayer' by rote," Stan says. "In fact, that's how I used to recite it too; it was just how we ended NA meetings. But now when I get to the phrase 'courage to change the things I can,' I'm almost stopped short by it. Because there's so much I *can* change. Not *control*. I still don't have a new job offer yet, even though I have some promising leads. All I have power over right now is who I send my resume out to, not how they respond to it. But I can also change my attitudes—about work, about other people, about myself. Which means I can let up on myself and allow whatever the world has in store for me to come through. That's really what it is: letting go so that life has a chance of coming to me."

What we discover in accepting this range of options is that we have the choice to change our minds. We don't have to adhere rigidly to any stance or attitude, relationship or self-view. This is a particularly important message third-year recoverers tell me they're learning about "working the program" of AA and NA. For many of us in the third year, the idea finally begins to sink in that Twelve Step programs are programs of suggestion, not coercion, with a great deal more latitude than we may have been prepared or willing to accept in our first or second year of sobriety.

Listen to some third-year recoverers talk about the program in the next section and you'll see what I mean.

four

What Does the Program Mean to Me Now?

Conversations with a wide range of people in their third year of recovery tell me that three main areas of the program cause the most consternation. The first one is simple: dealing with boredom. We've already heard William ask some basic and exasperated questions about going to meetings ("Do I have to do this for the rest of my life?"). A lot of people complain about hearing the same stuff over and over again at meetings or from their sponsors. From my observations, these are concerns that afflict both second- and third-year recoverers, but by the third year the problem can become intense enough to drive some people away from NA and AA, and sometime even back to drinking and drugging. Boredom with the program—with meetings, Twelve Step language, sponsors, AA and NA literature, and the rest of it—thus becomes something crucial to look into.

The second program-related issue third-year recoverers tell me about seems to arise from seeking solutions to the first. It amounts to the discovery that we are, after all (contrary to some common entrenched beliefs), *allowed to change our minds;* we can be flexible. Whether it's the prospect of changing sponsors, or the meetings you go to, or the way you approach the Steps, many of us in the third year feel a greater need to face our own inner rigidities and negative assumptions. We've already seen how people begin to view the world as wider, more abundant, and more full of choice than they had once believed it was. We'll see some third-year recoverers come to the same realization with regard to "working the program."

A third issue that comes up with more urgency by the third year has to do with believing that what you're learning in sobriety doesn't only apply to the good times; you can depend on program tools when you're going through rough stuff, too. Maybe this sounds obvious, but so many recovering men and women tell me that when they panic—when they go through periods of great upheaval, such as the death of a lover or parent or friend, the loss of a job, or other serious losses or illnesses—they clench. "I'm supposed to give up my will to God?" asks one horrified recovering woman who lost her job and is facing eviction proceedings because she hasn't been able to pay rent for six months. Learning that it's at *precisely* these times of need that the program can most help us is crucial, sometimes even life-saving.

The program, to recovering people in this book, covers a wide territory, but also a very rewarding one. As with just about everything else in recovery, there's more to this territory than you may think, sitting in yet another meeting, starting up, once again, at what one third-year recoverer refers to as "those same damned Twelve Steps."

Dealing with Boredom

Mel has been the whole mind-expansion route. "Sometimes I catch a glimpse of myself in a store window as I'm walking down the street and I feel a little foolish. Here I am, with a gray beard, hair over the back of my collar, a fifty-five-year-old man and dressed about the same way I was at thirty. Well," Mel laughs, "at least I've got a sense of humor about it. I don't have any illusions, anyway, about not looking like a superannuated hippie." Mel's eyes grow a little distant. "God, twenty-five years ago— just to think of it! My greatest period of euphoric recall lands me in about 1967, 1968. I bombed from coast to coast, from St. Mark's Place in New York to Haight-Ashbury in San Francisco. Couldn't get enough of what was going on. The Grateful Dead were my heroes. Acid, booze, reefer, mescaline, you name it, I did it."

Mel massages his forehead for a moment, as if to rub away the next, more perplexing mass of memories. "The problem, I guess, was I didn't stop when the rest of the world did. Not that I didn't become, you know, more corporate. The 'me decade' of the seventies, the whole business about looking out for Number One, gathering rosebuds while ye may—hey, I managed to cash in on that too. I joined est like everybody else. All the Eastern stuff, all my gurus, all the acid I'd done, all the sense I'd developed, right along with Mr. Leary, that the universe was a vast playroom where you could do anything you wanted to—it all deposited me in Mr. Erhard's lap. I've always been good with words too. Got some pretty lucrative jobs in the last ten or twenty years working in advertising for waterbed companies, an incense manufacturer, head shops. I actually managed to cash in on being a hippie, then being an est-head—I helped give those seminars, was one of the best people doing it too—then ushering in our current 'New Age.' But, you know, there was no center. Nothing had really happened to me inside. It's like my world was this confusing kaleidoscope, one brilliant whacked-out color after another, a kind of continuous acid trip on the surface of a bubble. Whenever you probed too deeply the bubble would pop. And I'd be hanging there, nothing but a few drops of mist. Nothing got through to me. It's like there was no me to get through *to*. Maybe this sounds all nice and Zen Buddhist, like I'd lost my ego and was on the way to Nirvana, but, shit, man, that wasn't it. For a long time I tried to think it was, tried to tell people that my complete inability to make a commitment to anything or anyone was evidence of my high spiritual development. But I was lying. There was *nothing* inside me by the end, by the time I knew I had to give up booze and drugs. I was a completely void shell of a man, with only enough nerve endings to feel an ache that wouldn't go away anymore, no matter what I did to myself to ease it."

Since Mel had turned into a virtual walking encyclopedia of spiritual self-help alternatives, he was no stranger to the existence of AA and NA. "I remember *New York* magazine ran an article about how trendy Twelve Step programs were becoming, the alternative they were offering to singles who didn't want to meet each other in bars anymore. I guess I was right on schedule, like I've always been. I started going to AA and NA, when publicity was especially high about it. You know, when all the movie stars were going to Betty Ford? I couldn't afford Mrs. Ford's facility, so, trendy boy that I couldn't help being, I went to some supposedly 'hot' meetings in Soho and the East Village in New York.

"And they took. I was in enough pain that something got through. The bubble hasn't burst, either. I can't begin to express my gratitude for the feeling that, for the first time in my life, I actually suspect I've got a *self*. Women I used to be involved with thought I was a sociopath, that I had no conscience, was constitutionally incapable of feeling anything about anyone. I almost believed them. But now I know they were wrong. I *am* capable of feeling things, of caring about other people, about myself. NA and AA have been godsends in that regard. And yet . . ."

Mel frowns; his voice softens. "As screwed up as I got on acid and booze and pot and the rest of it, it sure made life an intricate, busy, and pretty interesting affair, at least on the outside. I mean, I got used to things happening all the time. I'd move from home to home at the least provocation. Drop this woman for that woman, quit jobs in a great flurry of high drama, buy a new bed, go macrobiotic, then eat nothing but grapefruit, take off for India if I had enough credit on my Visa card to pay the plane fare. I was used to moving a lot. That euphoric recall I talked about can be a bitch. Sometimes I forget the despair at the center of all that activity. And so I go to a meeting and talk about it and usually it gets better; it comes back to me why it's so important right now to take things slower. But I've been taking them slower for nearly three years now, and the hard brutal truth is, I've gotten bored.

"Sometimes I just feel AA and NA are so limited. I mean, I know most of the literature we keep reading was written at a time in our culture when men's and women's roles were perceived much differently than they are now. There's a kind of implicit sexism in the Big Book and even the Steps themselves—which assume God is a 'Him'—that I know I'm not the first to notice. But it's more than that. It's like, all the stuff I've felt drawn to, all the meditation practices, the beliefs in past lives, exploring astral travel, all the magic and wonder and mystery of the universe that's always attracted me, maybe especially when I did acid and felt I could participate pretty directly in it—I want that to be a part of my life again too. But, shit, all I kept hearing in meetings was this prosaic stuff about 'One day at a time,' 'First things first,' and 'Keep it simple.' All good stuff, don't get me wrong, but I have *heard* that tune. I want some more stirring wisdom than that. I want to *fly*—like I used to."

Recently, at an AA meeting, somebody with about the same time in the program as Mel confessed that he didn't have a sponsor and that he thought he might like to get one. In his nearly three years of sobriety, Mel had never gotten a sponsor either. "I began to think that might be part of the problem. Along with being bored with the language that kept getting repeated in AA and NA, I had to admit I was getting bored with a lot of the people. I could accept that a lot of this was my doing. It's very hard for me just to *be* with someone. I always feel like I've got to perform. It was like a drug to me to get people to laugh when I spoke at a meeting; I loved it, but it was a performance. Not that it wasn't based on the truth. I had no need to lie, talking about my past. I had so many weird and colorful stories, there was no need to make anything up; all I had to do was pass it on intact! But, when I allowed myself to think of it, I'd never known one moment of real, unforced peace with another person—simply talking and listening without any real regard for the entertainment value. Maybe that was what I needed, and maybe the right sponsor could provide it."

Mel thus began a series of what he called "auditions." "I made a list of possible sponsors, guys with at least five years in the program, preferably people with ten or more. I started asking each one out for coffee after meetings. I was very meticulous, asking them what they thought the Steps were all about, how they helped other sponsees, whether they themselves had sponsors, the whole bit. (I may be New Age, but I'm pretty anal too.) After each coffee date I went home and wrote down some notes. Next to the list of names I'd prepared, I'd drawn two columns headed 'Pros' and 'Cons.' Joe would be 'easygoing' on the pro side, 'vague' on the con side. Pete would be 'conscientious' on the pro side, 'dogmatic' on the con. And so on. Then, finally, I met Steve."

Steve was a building contractor in New Jersey and, as Mel put it, "out of Central Casting; the perfect guy to play the part of a tough redneck conservative. Frankly, he was the last man I thought I could get along with as a sponsor. What would he make of my New Age stuff? The reason he was on my list was because every time I'd spoken in a meeting and he'd spoken after me, he'd said he identified with me. I was so intrigued that somebody like him could identify with me that I wanted to meet him."

Steve ended up being a lot more surprising than Mel ever anticipated. "That coffee date was something," Mel says. "Here I am sitting across from a big trucker-type guy with a crewcut, wearing a T-shirt and lumber jacket, muddy jeans and work boots, and I'm in my sandalwood beads and Indian-style loose shirt, bearded and long-haired—what a picture we made! But the amazing thing was, Steve turned out to be one of the most spiritually aware and provocative people I've ever met. And I mean *ever* met—that includes all those gurus back in the sixties. In that one meeting, he totally transformed my view of what the program was all about. It was like, you walk into a diner and you sit down and this construction worker starts telling you the meaning of the universe and you know he's *right*." Mel laughs. "And yet what he said wasn't at all in the clouds. It was real concrete—befitting his job, I guess! In fact, building was the metaphor he used. Basically he got me to see that AA and NA were programs that wouldn't work unless I found a way to accommodate *myself* to them. They were like empty houses, he said, that only had any use when you moved in and made them your home. Making them your home meant doing anything you damned well pleased, pretty much. There was, however, one taboo: The only thing that would bring down the whole house was picking up a drink or a drug. At that point, they couldn't provide you with much of anything. Everything you heard in the program, even everything you heard from AA's BMOC Bill Wilson, was meant as suggestions for furnishing the house. You weren't required to do it his way, or anybody else's. It was your house to do with what you pleased. However, you might want to entertain those suggestions like guests—hey, like the men I was interviewing as sponsors! I invite them in, give them a cup of coffee, talk a little bit, see what they're all about, see if I want them to come back again. That's how Steve said he approached the program, by 'trying it on for size.' In fact, the reason Steve liked what I had to say was because when he'd thought about it, 'tried it on for size,' he decided a lot of it fit. He'd even picked up this book I talked about, a book about Zen Buddhism, and spent the rest of our coffee date talking about it with me!"

Mel says he was "knocked over. But in a gentle way. Because I knew that what Steve was talking about was true, and it was what I needed to hear. The idea that what we're being offered by

Twelve Step programs is *suggestion* takes away all that police-mentality stuff I used to associate with organized religion or even some New Age spiritual groups: 'Do it my way or you're a failure.' I think that's what I was really reacting to, what my boredom was really about. My boredom was a kind of defense. I was resisting being coerced by the same old jargon. But now that I've given that up, which means now that I truly realize that no-body is trying to coerce me, the jargon has begun to speak to me in a new way. The first three Steps: Whew! I never realized how revolutionary they were. Take the Second Step, for example. Imagine truly coming to believe that a power greater than your-self could restore you to sanity. I could meditate on that for six years! It's like, beneath the familiarity and the repetitiousness of program language were whole unexplored worlds of possibility and meaning that were every bit as exciting and life-changing as any acid trip I'd ever taken. Only you took *this* trip in full con-sciousness. That's what made it so powerful. In sobriety, you were actually present in mind, body, and spirit. I hear the Steps and AA and NA slogans so differently now, as I go on. It's like I go through new levels of readiness and understanding; they mean different things every time I allow myself to think about them without resisting them. It's a whole new trip for me. A conscious trip. And it sure as hell isn't boring anymore."

Allowing Yourself to Change

Sobriety seems to be a softening process; recovering people with any amount of time in AA or NA teach me that the further we go in recovery, the greater our capacity to be receptive. Remember how Martha, two years after her mother's death, was finally able to feel love and forgiveness—not because she willed it, but be-cause something inside her developed to the point where she was ready to feel those things? Sooner or later, most recovering people come to the same realization: Insight and deeper understanding grow in a process that willpower can't force. Mel, too, realized that getting the most out of the program often meant not forcing or resisting what he heard out of fear and resentment. It helped equally to remember that all AA and NA were offering him was a series of suggestions, not requirements. "The more I think about it," Mel says, "not only boredom but resentment, anger, and depression are all emotional flags. They tell me I'm defending myself against something that terrifies me. Now I can allow myself to get down to what the fear is."

Loren says she knows how debilitating her fear can make her, and how rigidly defensive. "I suppose that's been the most difficult thing in my sobriety," she says. Loren says what she first resisted was the idea that she even belonged in AA, that she was alcoholic. "I'm glad I had the therapist I did," she says. "He suggested that AA was only one way of getting sober, and that I didn't have to label myself 'alcoholic' or 'addict' to benefit from it or any other route to recovery. It was only when I gave myself permission not to label myself 'alcoholic' that I could allow myself to sit in on an AA meeting. My story was very simple, not at all dramatic, and by no means did it put me in any gutter, or make me act completely out of control. I simply became aware that I got very depressed and anxious if I didn't have several glasses of wine every day after work or with dinner. I felt that I was verging on some kind of dependence, and that bothered me, but that was about as much as I was willing to admit. I certainly wasn't going to label myself a 'drunk.'"

Loren's defenses were all the way up at her first meetings, almost three years ago. "I winced when people talked about the horrible messes they'd gotten into drunk. More than once I wanted to walk out of the room. I didn't belong here! But, slowly, it became a habit to go—and I suppose I did, even early on, enjoy the humor and the camaraderie that blossomed in the early morning weekday meetings I went to. Something got to me, anyway. I certainly knew what depression felt like; a lot of the anxiety and fear that people talked about feeling in sobriety rang true for me. It was like, even if I couldn't quite accept that my history qualified me as 'alcoholic,' everything I heard about *recovery* seemed to be true enough for me. So I began to feel a little less alone or unique. But I still didn't say, "My name is Loren and I'm an alcoholic'; I kept it at, 'My name is Loren,' and I let people think what they wanted to."

As Loren allowed herself to listen, and to experience life without those three or four glasses of wine a day, her resistance to going to meetings decreased. "Those morning meetings were something I quickly grew to look forward to, even to depend on, in my first year. I saw them as the only oasis in my life. Everything else seemed to be getting worse. I'd never realized how much I needed that wine to help me through the night—to deal with my husband, to ease the tensions I'd felt during the day at work, to act as a sort of all-around reward for getting through the day. Now that I wasn't drinking, everything my husband did annoyed me. I was a powder keg at work too—it was like I couldn't control my temper when the least little thing didn't go my way. I started to depend on those morning AA meetings like a life raft. At least there I could vent how I felt! But as weeks and then months went by, and I passed my first-year 'birthday'—a year without a drink—and got well into my second, I started to get impatient. Part of it was my projection that everyone was impatient with *me*. I myself got sick of complaining about the same stuff day after day. Basically it all boiled down to my boorish, insensitive husband and my boorish, insensitive co-workers and the boorish, insensitive people I had to deal with in the rest of my life. My basic gripe involved why people weren't doing what I wanted them to do. There was no bottom to my resentments, to my capacity for frustration at what the 'Serenity Prayer' calls the things I cannot change.'"

Loren says she knew she was in a rut. "I had a sponsor whom I'd picked because she was pretty, docile, and passive. She reminded me of a girl I was friendly with back in high school, someone I knew I could make listen to me. I could just run on and on, venting my frustrations, and she wouldn't cut me off. But it wasn't helping. I'd read all the literature, the Big Book and the Twelve and Twelve and *Came to Believe*, the thing about spirituality. It was all very nice and I could draw more parallels to my own experience than I could when I first started going to meetings, but something in me wasn't really touched by any of it. My life was in a rut; that was all I knew. It's like, if I had a Higher Power, all it had done was seal my fate: I was stuck with my husband, with my job, with my home, with my life. None of it could ever change; it was all carved in granite, it had all been decided in advance by some unfeeling Fate. All I could do was hope for the occasional respite—a nice vacation, a good movie, and my AA friends to keep complaining to. Frankly, life was about as bleak as it had been when I drank. But then"—for the first time, Loren smiles and lets out a little laugh—"I started to pay more attention to Sal. Good old Sal. How I used to hate him."

Sal, Loren says, was a self-described "ornery cuss." "For nearly two years, he was the embodiment of everything I hated about AA. He talked about nothing but alcohol. When you tried to bring up something more psychological, he groaned. He was blunt and nasty. Our weekday meetings are all round-robin; we all get to share every morning, which means that over time we get to know one another pretty well. And I sure got to know Sal. Whenever it was his turn to speak, he almost always complained that people weren't talking enough about alcohol: 'I'm not here for therapy—I'm here to stay sober!' Sometimes all he'd say when his turn came was 'I'll pass,' rolling his eyes up to heaven. If he did talk at any length, it would be something like, 'I've never heard so much bullcrap in my whole life as I have heard this morning, and I won't dignify the proceedings with a response.' This frequently happened when I'd had one of my long-winded complaining sessions—which, as I said, was beginning to happen a lot. But the point is, Sal was a pain. I almost left that meeting a number of times, I couldn't stand him so much."

However, sometime in the middle of her second year, after taking a three-week vacation on a lakefront property she and her husband had rented ("It was torture, and especially bad because I really missed my morning meetings—I had no one to vent to."), Loren returned to find a significantly changed Sal. "I don't know—now that I think of it, maybe it wasn't so sudden. For a while before I left for vacation, Sal had been a little quieter, not so judgmental. Maybe it was my imagination, but I think I even caught him smiling once. But at first, when I got back from my vacation, I wasn't paying much attention to him. I was determined to dump all my rage and resentment, how incompetent my husband was, how miserable a time I'd had—I didn't care what Sal thought about it. So I really went into a tirade, and dumped it all. Sal, it happens, was sitting right next to me, and it was his turn to speak next. I steeled myself for the inevitable put-downs. But that's not what happened. He said, gently, 'I'm sorry to hear you're in so much pain. I feel like that a lot too. Sometimes I think my resentments will be the death of me.' And that was it. His voice gentle, almost caressing. Was this the same Sal? What on earth had happened to him?"

Loren chalked it up to a freakish mood change; surely he'd return to his old ornery self the next day. But he didn't. "It wasn't like he'd changed completely. I mean, he still made it clear that he wanted to hear about alcohol. But something hard to pin down had happened to him; he was just gentler. There was the tiniest touch of humor in his voice and his eyes when he railed in his familiar way about the 'self-appointed psychologists' in the room. And once he even said hello to me on the street. I'd passed him any number of times before and all I'd ever gotten from him was a stony glare. Something was changing. It was unnerving; I wasn't even sure I liked it! I was so used to the old nasty Sal. But as the weeks and then months went on, I began to pay more attention to this transformation. He started talking about his life, about his job washing dishes at a big hotel restaurant, how exploited he'd felt there. He talked about seeing his grown daughter for the first time in fifteen years. There were actually tears in his eyes!

"He was opening up—that's what was happening. And slowly it began to dawn on me that that's exactly what I hadn't allowed myself to do. I'd allowed myself to complain, but not to truly open up. Sal was talking about the pain in his life, but it had a sort of *hopeful* quality. It was like the point of talking about how he felt was to allow himself to heal. None of this was explicit. I'm only now searching for words to describe the mysterious process I saw him undergo. All I can tell you is that it had a kind of domino effect on me. As I saw Sal—Sal, the original monster of AA!—turn into a nice guy, as I heard him talk not only about the pain in his life but about the joy, like how happy he was to see his daughter again, I felt something begin to dislodge in me. It didn't happen overnight, God knows. In fact, I'm still, today, nearly three years in the program, only at the very beginning stages of it. But the net effect is, life isn't so terrible for me anymore. I'm actually, for the first time, beginning to understand what people mean when they identify themselves as 'gratefully recovering alcoholics.' I still can't quite bring myself, not even after all this time, to label myself 'alcoholic,' but I *have* started to say I'm gratefully recovering. It's like something inside me is getting warmer and more open. And I guess what I'm thinking on a very simple level is, if Sal can do it, so can I. What exactly is Sal doing? Getting better, I guess. Enjoying life more. Ceasing to judge everything and everybody so reflexively, so negatively. Being more humble. Like I said, if Sal can do all this, so can I. And, amazingly, that's what seems, slowly, to be happening. *I'm* getting better too."

Life, Loren says, is no longer carved in granite. "Whatever transformation is going on, it's giving me permission to see my life as much more open-ended. For example, until now I never truly realized you were allowed to change your mind!" Loren laughs. "I've been such a rigid control freak, such a fatalist, so critical—it was like every reaction I had only cemented me more in place. But now, the cement seems to be softening. I've allowed myself to change sponsors—and I've done it, I think, without hurting the first one. (Frankly, I think she was relieved to be rid of me.) I've even begun going to a few different meetings; somehow I never thought I was allowed to do that either, heaven knows why. It's like there's always been this loud naysayer in my head telling me, 'You can't change, you're not allowed to budge from where you are; once you've made a decision, that's it.' All of this turns out to be so untrue! I see that my whole premise used to be that I'm stuck right where I am, that there's no possibility of movement or growth. But now I am growing, and the 'pot' I'm in doesn't seem to be large enough to contain the roots anymore. Life is a different proposition than I thought it was. It's not something that traps you. Now it seems to be so much bigger and more accommodating."

Like a number of other third-year recoverers, Loren is discovering that changes that make growth possible are to be embraced, not feared. "I can still give myself a hard time," she says. "My head is still bound by so many old messages, so much negative crap that tells me I'll never change, I'll never be happy or live any kind of satisfying life. I know a lot of that comes from childhood, and I am learning not to trust what these old voices keep telling me. But I *am* learning to trust something growing right alongside all those old voices, something I pray will replace all that negativity. When I truly listen to and follow what I find in my own heart—and, admittedly, it can be hard sometimes to tell if the message is coming from my heart or my head—but when I'm convinced that I'm acting out of love for myself, not hate, my instincts turn out to be pretty good! It's so new for me, but I'm actually practicing being positive. And now that I'm looking at AA and meetings as a source of help to move on with my life, not just as a dumping ground for my resentments, there seems to be so much help to be had. The Steps are beginning to strike me as useful tools, not some kind of homework assignment to do grimly out of obligation. Maybe that sums it up: I'm starting to *want* to recover. The suggestions that AA gives me all seem, now, to be coming from a loving urge to help me, not to keep me in line. This is still all so new. But it feels like, as long as I keep going to meetings, as long as I don't let myself retreat into that old self-hatred, I'm on a wonderful road. I don't know where it's taking me; I only know that it feels right to be traveling on it. I have so much more hope than I ever did before."

Loren laughs again, "Thanks, in large part, to the ornery cuss Sal."

Taking It to the Program

Most recovering people eventually learn that Twelve Step programs offer tools to help you get better, not a series of sledgehammers to beat yourself up with or a cage to keep you in line. But it can still be hard, when the going gets really rough, to believe that you can "trust in a Higher Power" to take care of you, or depend on AA or NA to pull you through.

Scott and Meg live in Miami Beach and have been married for five years. Scott says he is so grateful—"awed would be as good a word"—that Meg stuck by him, not only during the last and worst days of his drinking and drugging, but through the very rocky first months and years of sobriety. "I love her more than anyone in the world. I know that spouses of alcoholics and addicts get a bad rep—it's like they're automatically labeled 'codependent' just for hanging in there. But Meg isn't pathologically connected to me, or anyone else. She's one of the most well-adjusted people I know." Scott smiles. "Of course, that's a problem sometimes. I often think we come from different planets:

It's amazing how differently nonalcoholics and nonaddicts can see the world! They simply aren't compulsive in the same way we are—or I am, anyway. But Meg goes to Al-Anon, thank heaven, so she gets some help for herself, and a lot more understanding of what's going on with me."

Scott, at thirty-two, has been sober for about two and a half years. "Basically, I got high on a lot of cocaine and a fair amount of above-average quality—you know, 'vintage'—wine. I guess you could say I was a yuppie, or wanted to be one anyway. I had all sorts of illusions about being the next big thing to hit real estate," he says. "I was going to be Florida's Donald Trump, but I'd succeed where Trump had failed. Miami Beach's Deco district was just coming back to life; I was sure the sky was the limit! Of course, the job I had was barely more than assistant to a realtor— my grandiose plans took place mostly in my head. Cocaine helped—it made me feel like a king—and wine brought me down to a nice comfortable buzz. Or at least it used to. By the time I met and married Meg, it was all turning me into a paranoid mess.

"Meg was a secretary in the real estate firm where I worked. She had no illusions about me being a model of mental health. She says she knew I was 'troubled,' but that she saw something in me that had nothing to do with whether or not I was going to be a raging success. She said she saw a good heart." Scott pauses, almost in tears. "God knows how she saw that. I was so cut off from any feelings. But maybe the one good part left in me responded to her, and I fell in love, as much as I *could* fall in love, whacked out as I was. I was still able to hide the extent of my drug use; I don't think Meg would have married me otherwise. Honestly, she's never been on a self-destructive kick. But once she saw how hooked I was, she didn't automatically bolt. Not that she knew what to do, at first, except to offer me a lot of love. Well, one thing she did was start going to Al-Anon. And as great as I know that was for her, when she told me what she was doing, I lost it. I was drinking and snorting coke pretty much non-stop that day, and I was anxious that I wouldn't have enough to get me through the night. I was in more than my usual paranoid rage, and when she told me about going to Al-Anon, I nearly broke a chair over her head. How dare she think I was an alcoholic or addict! She fled, in tears, and I was left with the memory of having nearly killed the only person in my life I loved. I decided at that moment that I needed help."

Meg came back when she was convinced that Scott was serious about recovering, and, as Scott says, "I couldn't ask for a more supportive partner, now that I'm sober." But Scott's sobriety hasn't marked the total turnaround he'd hoped for in their lives. "I was thrilled when Meg got pregnant two years ago—well, thrilled and scared. I loved the idea that we were going to have a baby together, have a real family. But the fact that I was sober hadn't turned me into the great success I wanted and, more than that, thought I *deserved* to be." While Miami Beach's real estate market was indeed being resuscitated, Scott seemed to be jinxed. "I couldn't understand it. I was so sure that now that I was off drugs and booze and in recovery and working my program, everything would magically get better. But my real estate firm got bought by some big outfit from New York and they totally revamped, bringing down a lot of their guys and kicking me, Meg, and several other Miami Beach natives out on our asses." Scott just couldn't seem to get another job in the field. "At first I thought, hey, I'm in my first year of sobriety: Take it slow. Things will work out. But then I was in my second year. And now I'm in my third year. And my life feels just as stuck now as it did back then. I managed to get this or that job, and for a while, after the baby got a little bigger, Meg was doing some freelance word processing when she could find an affordable baby-sitter. But we're *poor*, damn it; there's no other word for it. And now we're both out of work again. It's like my Higher Power has been putting me through some kind of test. If so, I'm not sure anymore that I can pass it. I've really started to feel that this can't go on much longer."

Scott and Meg's problems aren't only financial. "Our baby girl was born with a weak heart. It was really touch and go for the whole first year of her life. And she's still not out of the woods. The medical bills have been staggering. We had to move out of a fairly nice place we lived in when we had more money; now we're down in a lizard- and roach-infested hot little apartment in a crummy section of South Beach. The air conditioner keeps breaking down. Boy, you don't know what hot is till you're with a screaming baby in a tiny apartment at noon in the middle of July in Miami Beach."

His tone turns pleading. "I thought self-esteem was supposed to get better in sobriety! But mine has plummeted to about zero." Scott says it doesn't help that, although he's always had dreams of great success, his family background taught him to expect the opposite. "I'm from a poor, working-class, alcoholic family. I now realize that when I don't have money, there's some voice inside me that says, 'What do you expect? You're a loser from a no-good family. Being poor is what you deserve.' So I get into a big self-pity trap. No money, a sick baby, an impossibly hot apartment—and then, right before Christmas, just weeks ago, Meg's mother died."

Meg's mother was her only living relative; her father had died when Meg was a baby and she had no brothers or sisters. Scott says Meg had adored her mother, "and, frankly, her mother was a big help to us. She always took care of the baby. She helped with some of the medical bills. She was a good lady; it's no secret where Meg got her own good nature and fortitude. The most horrible thing was, she keeled over with a heart attack right in front of Meg in our kitchen. It was a terrible shock. Christmas was just a couple of weeks away. She was putting up a string of Christmas cards, which was one of our few decorations that year. And she collapsed."

Christmas promised to be a bleak affair. "I've never felt more like doing coke and drinking," Scott says. "I remember leaving Meg for a moment at the funeral home where she was making arrangements for her mother's burial, and walking across to the ocean, by all the pastel-colored hotels, the soft, warm air blowing in over the water, the tanned, beautiful people sitting at the outdoor bars, laughing and drinking. Here we were, broke, going through the death of Meg's mother, struggling with a sick baby in a small, stifling apartment, with no prospects that I could see for any of it getting better. And I was sober. Big frigging deal, I thought. I don't know what kept me from spending my last few dollars on a drink at one of those bars. But I didn't. I returned to Meg. We somehow got through what we had to do about her mother's funeral, and went home."

A week before Christmas, after Meg's mother's funeral, Scott and Meg tried to face the holiday for the sake of their daughter, Carol. "Meg's mother had given us her artificial Christmas tree, ornaments, and lights; she'd wanted to make sure Carol saw a big, beautiful tree that year. So even though we had no heart for it, we put it up, decorated it, strung the lights—all while dealing with our screaming two-year-old baby. The depression, the heat—it was a hot December—the noise: We'd just about had it. Finally, Carol calmed down a little, the tree was up, and Meg and I just collapsed into the couch. We both looked up at the tree, which really did look nice. 'Mama would have wanted us to enjoy this,' Meg said. Our daughter was in a better mood and was getting curious about this colorful big thing in the middle of the room. 'Turn the lights on,' Meg told me. So I did. And it was beautiful. So beautiful that Carol went stumbling off Meg's lap and ran to the tree, grabbing on to one of the lights. The second she touched it, the lights went out. This was the last straw for Meg. 'I'd wanted us to sit here later on, the baby in bed, just you and me and the tree, just for *one* moment of peace.' Meg started to cry. Carol started screaming again: She couldn't understand why the brightly lit tree had grown so dark. Meg wearily brought her into our bedroom, where she sleeps in a crib, and I faced the tree.

"I don't know that I've ever felt worse despair than I felt in that moment. Why did we keep ramming into all these brick walls? Why had *nothing* gone right for us, no matter what we did, day after day, month after month, year after year? It was like that movie *It's a Wonderful Life*—except that no guardian angel was coming down to cheer me up. And anyway, Jimmy Stewart wasn't a coke head. Cocaine—damn, that would at least lift my spirits a little. I started to crave it again. Really crave it. I remember hugging myself for a moment, listening to Meg in the next room cooing to our daughter, trying to get her to stop crying. I closed my eyes and for that moment really wished I was either high or dead. Then I opened my eyes and looked over at the tree. I suddenly saw why the lights had gone out: The plug had been loose and had fallen out of the socket. It was just a coincidence that the lights went out when Carol touched them."

Scott plugged in the cord again and the lights came back on. Something else was illuminated too. "I know it sounds corny. Some combination of Scrooge 'seeing the light' and that *Wonderful Life* movie. But putting the plug back into the socket filled me with a strange kind of joy and hope. *There was something I could do.* It was like, plugging those lights in was the first real, positive action I'd taken all day. And this put a thought into my head that I couldn't remember having had for so long: Maybe there are things I can do to make things better. Maybe it's wrong to give up hope just when we need hope the most."

Scott couldn't really articulate the feeling to Meg, but it stayed with him the next day when he went to his NA meeting. "Everyone was talking about holiday anxiety: a big hurdle for us addicts and alcoholics. But I was hearing people differently. Before, I'd always felt like nobody had it as bad as me. But now I saw that a lot of people had problems, problems they had no idea how to deal with. I saw that maybe, just maybe, I could try 'turning it over' again—keeping my eyes open, plugging in the lights when required, doing all I could to keep going. Maybe the thing that had been lacking for all these months was that I never really asked for guidance. Spiritual guidance. I'd always sort of glossed over that part of recovery. I'd seen the Eleventh Step, about seeking 'through prayer and meditation to improve our conscious contact with God *as we understood Him,*' and I thought, yeah, it really is nice to calm down a bit, meditate, bliss out. But I'd never seen that spiritual process as especially practical, or something I urgently needed to do. Now it felt both practical *and* urgent: I felt the hunger to reach out like I'd never reached out before. Just acknowledging that has brought me a new feeling of peace and hope. It suddenly seems awfully premature to give up. Life has so much more in store for me and my family. And I know now in my heart that we'll be able to handle it and grow from it and things will get better. I suppose my feeling now is that things will get better once I come to a bit more inner peace, and, of course, if I keep looking for a job."

We often hear in AA and NA meetings that all recovery is spiritual. In the third year, a lot of recovering alcoholics and addicts seem to come to a new and deeper understanding of this. Every person's story in this book seems to teach us that moments of new illumination, of deeper insight and understanding, don't come as the result of willing them into being. They come through the backdoor. They come as a kind of natural product of our recovery. Staying away from alcohol and drugs, going to meetings, and talking and listening to other recovering people seem to prepare us for a kind of inner growth and new receptivity. As we've seen, sobriety softens us. Rigid and negative self-views and assumptions about how the world works seem, eventually, to slough off like obsolete skins, skins we grow out of because they've outlived their usefulness. As Loren said, "The pot I'm in doesn't seem to be large enough to contain the roots anymore."

As we've also seen, as long as we don't drink or drug there's no forcing or holding back this growth. Whatever timetable we're on, it isn't susceptible to petition; we can't seem to speed it up, or hold it back, by any act of will. But slowly, for so many people I've talked to who are in their third year of sobriety, a more patient sense of self emerges, a sense in which "turning it over" is completely consonant with exerting all your willpower in the service of what your heart and your Higher Power tell you you deserve to have. A new sense of accountability, not blame, grows in us, a better clarity about the enigma of the Serenity Prayer. We slowly grow to see what we've got the power to change and what we don't. Finger pointing and guilt mongering, as Martha taught us, aren't productive anymore. Sobriety seems to lead us to a new curiosity about how life *works*, not to new ways of blaming this or that circumstance or person for why it's not working.

So much of what we learn in the program has to do with identifying our own complicity in what happens in our lives. We learn not to beat ourselves up for the blocks and imperfections we inevitably find in ourselves, but to see our circumstances in a nonjudgmental way in order to have a better chance of creating the life we want to live. People in their third year of recovery have much to tell us about what it can be like to live responsibly and to be accountable, which (to the astonishment of a lot of recovering people) has nothing to do with guilt or blame.

fïve

Where's the Villain?
A New Sense of Accountability

"Okay," sighed a friend of mine who's in his third year of sobriety, after reading this far. "It is a relief to hear from Geraldine, William, Scott, Martha, and all those other people that guilt and shame are pretty unproductive. When I think of things I've done wrong or ways I've really harmed other people, and I beat myself up over it, it just makes it worse, keeps me stuck in the mud. But something still doesn't quite make sense to me. What about the stuff I still have to make amends for? How is feeling accountable different from feeling guilty? I can't always distance myself from the chaos I've brought into my life. My guilt is so reflexive, I can't always stave it off. How is it possible to look at the mess you've made of your life and not feel terrible about it?"

Recovering people I've met across the country, and especially recovering people in their third year of sobriety, echo my friend's discomfort, which is often felt and expressed as no less than self-hate. As we amass more time in recovery and get more familiar with what the program variously (depending on whether it's the Fifth, Sixth, or Seventh Step) calls our "wrongs," "defects of character," and "shortcomings," it's hard to remain in the company of all these "wrongs" without feeling pretty terrible about having committed them. "The fact is," my friend says, "I still don't really like myself much. That's what I keep getting down to when I try to do a Fourth Step. How could anyone who's done the awful stuff I've done in my life—not only drunk and high, but sometimes even in sobriety—think of himself as anything *but* a terrible person? Yeah, I know, I hear a lot about how you have to forgive yourself, learn to accept and love yourself. But a lot of times those are just empty words to me. I'm stuck with some pretty incontrovertible evidence that I'm a selfish, cowardly loser. How am I supposed to forgive all that?"

The Fearless Journey

Exploring this area of guilt versus accountability, as my friend suggests, is generally quite painful. Len, who has nearly three years in NA and AA, has found the question of forgiveness especially knotty. But in his attempt to grapple with that question, he's come up with some insights that may help my friend and the rest of us who think there's no way out of the self-hate that the very prospect of "a fearless moral inventory" may provoke in us.

At thirty years old, Len is a wiry and, as he puts it, "counter culture kind of guy" from a small town in Ohio. He went to college at a very progressive school, a school in which he developed some fiercely held political beliefs. "I was pretty grandiose, I guess. I felt God had sort of loosed me upon the world to make a difference. What that difference was going to be, I'm not sure. But throughout high school and college I'd always gravitated to causes. Nuclear disarmament, saving the earth—any number of political things. I think I was jealous of the generation before me, the guys who marched against the Vietnam War. I came out of a whole different era, where it seemed that we had so much less power to affect anything, change anything, make anything better. But maybe I was projecting. I majored in psychology in college, and, God help me, I've never been the same since I learned about the superego. It was like, from the moment I identified it,

I'd found my enemy! Any police-sounding voice in my head was suspect. I reacted to my conscience as if it were an overbearing parent: 'Don't tell *me* what to do!' I now know that a lot of my attraction to vast causes and political movements all came out of this—a personal sense of powerlessness about not being able to direct my own life. The only relief from this feeling of impotence was pot, booze, and sex. Which all were pretty much bound up in one another."

Len's naively sweet nature could turn wickedly cruel when he got drunk and high. "I was a classic Jekyll and Hyde," he says. "It's really hard for me to admit what I was like when I got out of control. For one thing—and this isn't something I feel I can talk about in the rooms, but I'm working on it in therapy and with my sponsor—my sexual fantasies got really violent. I met this woman in college who drank and smoked as much pot as I did, and we had a really sick, abusive relationship. It was a physically violent one, and the violence only made us more turned on. We never hurt each other badly, but we came close. I can't go into details about it; it's still awfully hard to face. But it let loose in me a kind of sadomasochistic 'head' that still torments me now. For years, I'd espouse peace and love and tolerance, then get drunk and stoned and find—sometimes pay—partners to act out my 'dark side,' the sinister black-leather fantasy side. Hell, I majored in psychology; I know this is some kind of eroticized rage. All the anger I've got buried inside me has to come out somehow. It's like a problem in physics: When energy builds up enough, something will blow. Well, what triggered the explosion for me was booze and drugs. And I grew to depend on that trigger until it pretty much blotted out everything else in my life. It wasn't enough to pour my anger into socially acceptable causes. I had to do it in sex too. And, boy, did I."

When Len got sober, which he did after a particularly frightening sexual experience in which he got so drunk that he blacked out—and woke up on the floor to find a hastily scribbled note next to him from his partner that read, 'I never want to see you again. If you even try to see me I'll call the police'—he hoped that the "Hyde" part of him had finally been put to rest. "For the first six months, I really did calm down inside," Len says. "I was so blasted by the relief of not being hungover, of feeling better—it was like some childlike part of me was allowed to wake up and blink at the light. It was easy for me to take things slow. To enjoy the simple things in life. I really felt I'd regained some kind of innocence. It was such a relief!" But as he got physically better, the old emotional 'dark side' began rearing its head again. "I heard someone in an AA meeting once say that it's easy to help an alcoholic when he first comes into the rooms and he's desperate for help. But it's hard to help an alcoholic when he's got a little sobriety and he feels better. He's just not as hungry for help and doesn't realize he continues to need as much help. That pretty much sums up how I felt as I got better. It wasn't that I stopped thinking I was an alcoholic and addict. My past had made it too clear that I was. But the sexual stuff, and the anger, all started to come back. And this time it was excruciating. Because I was *conscious* now. I never realized how much guilt I was capable of feeling!"

Len would sometimes pick up pornographic magazines that ran personal ads and fantasize about the ones that seemed to clue into his old S & M fantasies. "Sometimes I'd write letters to those women and then tear them up into little pieces, swearing I'd never do it again. I remember making myself crazy with a sexual fantasy about a particular ad, writing out a three-page pornographic response, just going wild, and then hating myself so much that I took the letter into the woods, burned it, and buried it in the mud, in some kind of ritual exorcism! It was like there were two me's: the horrendous evil sexual me, and the sweet good-natured well-meaning sober angelic me. It was that neatly divided. But the division was pulling me apart. You can't know how horrible it was for me to face what I hated about myself, especially because I felt so completely powerless over it. Nothing seemed to help. I'd do anything—go to more meetings, take walks, take cold showers, force myself to read the Big Book, call up people, try to make myself think of other stuff—but nothing worked. I couldn't get away from the dark half of me."

By the middle of this second year, Len began to resent sobriety. "What was being sober doing for me except making it clear what a hateful person I was? I'd taken all the suggestions the program and my sponsor gave me. I did a lot of service, made coffee, ran meetings. In fact, once when my home group was having an anniversary party and they needed people to volunteer to bring food, I spent two whole days making salads and baking pies. I pretty much catered the damned thing single-handedly! I had three sponsees by my second-year 'birthday.' I felt guilty if I saw that anything needed doing. I volunteered for everything. I was your model recovering addict and alcoholic. But the inside stuff, the dark 'Hyde' half, wouldn't go away. In fact, it tormented me more, and made me feel more like a fraud. If anyone knew what I was really like, what was really going on in my head, they'd have run out screaming."

Len's sponsor, Mark, knew he was troubled, but he wasn't able to get Len to talk about what was troubling him. "I was really evasive with Mark. And I know Mark knew I was hiding. He kept trying to get me to do a Fourth Step. I kept telling him I wasn't ready. But he kept at me. Finally, one day when we both were at a point of exasperation—and I mean I was about ready to tell him to shove it, and drop him as a sponsor if he didn't stop talking about the Fourth Step—Mark said something that got through to me. 'Do you know what the word "fearless" means?' he asked me. I'd had it up to here with what I called his 'damned coercive tactics.' But I told him, yeah, I knew what the hell "fearless" meant. I spoke English, didn't I? It meant brave. I remember laughing a little. 'Brave,' I thought to myself. 'You want to come up with a word for what I'm not? You got one right there.' Mark took a deep breath. 'It doesn't mean brave,' he said. 'It means *without* fear.'"

Len says that something about this definition got his notice. "I think Mark saw that my defenses opened up a bit. It was like something out of *Star Trek*—you know, when for a moment the spaceship's shields let up and it's suddenly vulnerable?" Len laughs. "Anyway, Mark dove right in, phasers at full tilt. He said that what always used to clench him about the Fourth Step—about writing down that 'fearless moral inventory'—was that he used to think it meant having to be brave, that you had to have a huge amount of courage. 'And, man,' Mark said, 'if there's one thing I knew I was it was chicken. How could I write down, and then tell anybody else, all the lousy stuff I'd done in my life? I was sure I didn't have it in me. But then I got to thinking. Did I really need to be brave? I calmed down and looked at that word *fearless* again. Suddenly it came to me that its literal meaning didn't have anything to do with bravery. Brave meant standing up against something horrible, testing your mettle against something that threatened to engulf you, maybe even kill you! Like fighting some kind of huge fire-breathing dragon—that's what brave meant. But *fearless* meant not having any fear. And I began to wonder, was there ever a time when I felt like that? Any time since I've been sober? Then it came to me. *Yes—the moment I surrendered to the realization that I was an alcoholic and an addict.* For me, that was the greatest moment of peace and fearlessness I've ever known. It didn't *matter* what I had done up until that moment. All I knew was that I needed help and I would go to any lengths to get it. It was a spiritual thing. I saw that I wasn't a hateful person. I was a person in pain and in need. Even with all the stuff I'd done to hurt myself and other people, it didn't mean I was a hateful person. It became clear to me that what I needed to do was offer it all up. That was the feeling: All I had to do was give it up to something.

"That's what Mark said he was trying to encourage me to do

too. To surrender. Whatever it was that was bothering me, it didn't make me a horrible human being. It just made me human." Len frowns, remembering how frustrated he'd felt at that moment. "At first, I couldn't register what he was saying. I mean, something about it caught my attention, like I said. I guess because I also knew what that moment of surrender felt like. Mine didn't come in a great huge flash like it seemed to have come for Mark, but when I was ready to put down booze and drugs, it was a real feeling of having had enough. I knew, sort of, that was *it*. I was at the end of my rope. And so I started to wonder, am I at the end of this other rope too? The rope of hating myself for my fantasies, for my 'Hyde' half? At first I wasn't sure. But I knew it was possible to look at all of this a bit differently. I could begin to explore the blackness, all this dark, violent stuff in me. The idea began to grow, I guess, that maybe I didn't have to *judge* it all so harshly.

"The light I'm allowing on the parts of me I had always hidden is dim. But I've started to tell Mark the truth. Kind of trotting out this and that specific detail about my sexual history to see what kind of effect it might have on him. He didn't freak. In fact, he shared some dark stuff about his own past with me. And I began to understand what 'fearless' felt like. This wasn't as hard as I thought it would be. Mark was right. It wasn't a question of being brave. Sure, there's still the need for courage in my sobriety. Sometimes just getting up in the morning and facing a new day takes a lot of it! But making progress about the secret stuff in me I didn't dare to tell anybody—I'm discovering that takes something a little different. It takes something closer to surrender. Once you've surrendered, once you've given it up, what's there to be afraid of? You've let it go. You don't have to keep hiding or running from it anymore. That's what fearless feels like."

Allowing himself to see his "Hyde half" in this new context has, much to his amazement, allowed Len to begin writing his

Fourth Step. "I'm taking it slow. But I no longer expect my pen to burn a hole in the page. I'm getting closer to the idea that the goal here is clarity about myself, not self-denigration. And, boy, you can't imagine how far *that* is from what I used to feel." A dividend for Len as he goes through his inventory is that the whole notion of accountability seems less charged. "I'm starting to see my life more in terms of cause and effect than as good or evil. When I felt certain ways and did certain things, what was the result? How did it make me feel? What effect did it have on the people around me? It becomes a more clinical problem than I ever thought it could be. And the program is so reassuring. The Fourth and Fifth Steps don't tell me I have to rush out and correct everything. All they suggest is that I find out what's going on, and let somebody else know about it. That's difficult for me to register. I mean, like a lot of other recovering alcoholics and addicts I've listened to, when I get a feeling, I think I've got to act on it. So when I start to get a little clearer about how certain people, places, and things affect me, my first impulse is usually to run out and change everything. Quit my job, get out of my relationships, move to a different city. But that's not what this process is about. It's those three A's I hear about in meetings: awareness, acceptance, and, down the road a piece, action. The Fourth and Fifth Steps have to *do* with the first A: awareness. I don't have to rush and do anything about all this stuff yet."

Len says that another unanticipated dividend from engaging in this fearless work is that he's easing up on himself in a good deal of the rest of his life. "I'm no longer taking myself quite so seriously. And I have more of the feeling that I'm taking care of myself. Yeah, that's probably the best part of this. I actually feel that, in this attempt to take a nonjudgmental look at myself, I'm taking care of myself. In fact, when I think about it, I'm automatically taking better care of myself when I don't. I'm not inflicting any more wounds. Like that thing about hitting yourself with a hammer because it feels so good when you stop? Well,

I've stopped—at least sometimes—hitting myself with that hammer, and damn, it *does* feel better."

Another Surprise in Recovery:
Getting Physical

Len's feeling of taking care of himself is hard won. It means going against deeply ingrained negative reflexes. Many third-year recoverers tell me about similar awakenings. Once you have had some experience getting through each day for a few years without drugs and alcohol, you begin to *want* to take care of yourself, and not only emotionally. Taking care of ourselves physically often becomes equally appealing in sobriety. But this, too, means facing a lot of fears and hurdles.

"I suppose it's pretty obvious," Sonia laughs. "I mean, I can't make myself *go away* anymore like I used to when I got high! And after enough days, weeks, months, and years of seeing I'm still here, awake, conscious of my life in ways I've never been before, it occurs to me that I'd better take better care of this self I keep bumping into." In her mid-forties, Sonia is a social worker who helps the homeless. "I spent most of my drinking and drugging days trying to help other people stop drinking and drugging. Many of the people I work with are alcoholics and drug addicts. There isn't a social agency, rehab, or clinic in the state that deals with addiction that I can't give you chapter and verse about. But not once did it occur to me that I could make use of this information."

Sonia finally decided to try to get sober when her live-in boyfriend, who "had been hooked on everything from Dom Perignon to crack," decided *he* had had enough. "My boyfriend, Chris, was such a mess that by comparison I seemed to be completely normal. Wasn't I working with alcoholics and addicts? There had been no reason to think of myself as having a problem with drinking and drugging. I still had a job. My life was still manageable—well, as manageable as it could be living with a nut like Chris and doing the kind of work I do. But when Chris got sober, I couldn't get over the change in him. It made me face a lot of stuff in my own life, especially when he got out of rehab and said he didn't think he could live with me if I continued to drink and drug."

It took a few false starts, "during which I had to realize I was getting sober for *me,* not to hold on to Chris," but Sonia finally did achieve that moment of surrender. "Chris and I were like two children in a sandbox," Sonia said. "I mean, the whole world was different now that we weren't getting wasted every day. Fighting, making love, cooking dinner, talking to each other—it was like a whole new planet. I wasn't always sure we could stay with each other. Frankly, I'm still not always sure about this. It's a strange thing to have lived with someone for so long and suddenly discover that you really don't know him at all—and here you are waking up in the same bed! But we're working at it. I've got to find out who I am in order to be in any real position to see who Chris is. And that has not been an entirely delightful process.

"When I stopped drinking and drugging, I started eating. Eating really bad stuff: greasy fried chicken, fast-food hamburgers and fries. I've heard a lot of other recovering addicts say in meetings that the void we stuffed with drugs and alcohol doesn't go away when we stop drinking and drugging. I gained forty-five pounds in my first year. It freaked me out; I've been a little plump before, but never *fat.* I started getting severe stomach cramps after about ten months in the program. And other physical stuff began going wrong: strange rashes out of nowhere, an inability to sleep. And toothaches—God, when you can't numb it with brandy or pills, a toothache is a nightmare! It was like, in sobriety, my body was staging a revolt. Part of it, I told myself, was just detoxing from all the crap I'd shoved into myself for so many years. But the biggest surprise was acknowledging that my self—including my physical self—wouldn't go away. For a long time, I tried to do what I'd always done when I drank and drugged: ignore what was going on until it went away. I became aware that my usual tactic for dealing with anything unpleasant was to avoid it. But it wasn't working anymore; my body wouldn't let me ignore what was going on. So I started to project all sorts of horrible things. That I had liver cancer, or that some terrible rare disease was causing my rashes. I've always had a morbid fear of going to the doctor. Both my parents died of cancer, and as a child, every time they went to a doctor's appointment, I was afraid they wouldn't come back. Doctors meant death to me."

However, Sonia became so physically uncomfortable, and so difficult to live with because of it, that Chris made a doctor's appointment for her. "Chris said that *he* had a doctor's appointment, and asked me to go with him. When Chris finally admitted that he'd made the appointment for me, not him, I nearly hit him! How dare he trick me like this! But when I calmed down, I felt a little relieved. I really *was* worried about my health, and I was ready for help."

Sonia's willingness only went to a certain point, however. "I agreed to a general checkup. I mean, I knew that wouldn't mean a whole lot more than a few pokes, prods, and a cold stethoscope on my chest and back. But when the doctor said he wanted to do a few more tests, I freaked. What did he think was wrong? What awful diseases did he suspect me of having? Was I going to die? Is that what he couldn't bring himself to tell me? Chris was still in the room, and the doctor said to him, 'We've got a real *case* here, don't we, Chris?' He reassured me that these tests were a part of a normal checkup procedure, just some standard blood and urine work. So I went through with it."

Sonia's medical tests were gratifyingly undramatic. She needed to lose weight; her blood pressure was a bit high, but a better diet would help; she was slightly allergic to dairy products; her liver and kidneys were okay; she could benefit from several trips to the dentist. But the effect on her was profound. "Going to the doctor became proof that I *existed.* Maybe this sounds weird, but even in sobriety, I still didn't want to accept that I had a body, that what I did to my body had an effect on it. You'd think I would have gotten that message from giving up alcohol and drugs. I did, in a way; certainly I was aware of not having hangovers or being strung out all the time. But after I'd adjusted to that, I reverted to thinking of my body, when I thought of it at all, as something cosmetic, something I could make look good enough to attract Chris to make love to me, or presentable enough to go out to dinner, or serviceable enough to get me through the day. Like clothing, I suppose. Not very important. In fact, sort of distasteful.

"I remember feeling this very strongly when I smoked dope in the old days, and I remember thinking, 'God, what a wonderful, spiritual person I am—I don't care about my body!'" Sonia laughs. "But now I was beginning to see that my body was *me*; it was something I had a responsibility to take care of. Seeing that doctor helped me break through a tremendous wall of fear. I still freak out at the thought of going to a doctor; that's a lifelong phobia it'll take more than one checkup to get past. But it helped me to shift my perspective about myself. I *do* have a body. It's a gift, something to cherish, something to take care of." Sonia laughs again. "I still talk about it in the abstract, as if it's not quite *me*, don't I? I haven't fully moved into my physical self, that's pretty obvious. But something about my attitude has changed. Taking care of myself isn't only meditating or thinking positive thoughts. It isn't only an emotional or intellectual process. It's a physical process too."

Nearing her "third birthday" in AA and NA, Sonia has gone to the dentist a couple of times. "I've been as afraid of dentists as I have been of doctors. I had to talk about these fears a lot with my recovering friends before I could even think of making an appointment. But thank God I did. I'm convinced that the Two T's terrify us more than anything: teeth and taxes. It's amazing how tied to self-esteem teeth seem to be. It's such a source of shame for so many people, but such a triumph when we muster the courage even to talk to a dentist about it. I always projected that whatever dentist I went to would turn into some awful moralistic authority: 'How could you *do* this to yourself, you horrible stupid evil person?' But these fears turn out to be false. Nobody's out to tear me down. I'm the one who does that. They don't stand in judgment. But even if they did, so what?"

Physical health is new to recovering people, and fears about addressing it appear to be endemic. Hal, an accountant with two and a half years of sobriety, is astonished that "number one, I care enough about myself to want to get health insurance, and, number two, I can ask people about how a sixty-year-old self-employed man with a history of liver trouble can *get* health insurance without going bankrupt." Learning to take this kind of care of himself is, he says, "a miracle. I used to swig vodka whenever anything hurt. My solution to everything was to blot it out. I can't tell you what a leap it is to go out of my way to spend money on health care."

Other third-year recoverers join gyms or start to jog or exercise. "It's like my body is slowly materializing," says Suzanne, a young woman with twenty-six months in NA. "Like in *The Invisible Man*. My flesh is becoming visible, palpable, present. This isn't so wonderful, by the way. My self-esteem has been so low for so long that my first response to my body is generally 'Ugh!' I hate how I look a lot of the time. But I'm starting to accept that I'm *here*. And maybe I'm starting to enjoy the fact that there are some things I've got control of, physically. How much and what I eat, for example. What kind of exercise I might actually like to do. Getting medical checkups. But the best thing is, I'm not the first person who's ever had this problem. Everyone I listen to at meetings talks about this stuff all the time. It's like there's nothing I'm going through that somebody else hasn't had experience with. And when I don't hear it by sitting in a meeting waiting to hear it, I can ask questions."

This amounts to a new sense of accountability, similar to what Len learned to accept in his mental and emotional life. Alcoholism and addiction are spiritual, mental, and physical diseases, and so are our means of recovering from them. Accepting that we are physical beings is as necessary to recovery as accepting our spiritual and mental selves.

The spiritual self usually ends up providing the fuel for the rest of life. Allie, a twenty-nine-year-old aspiring actress in Los Angeles, has had to face some harsh physical realities about getting back into shape for work after years of ruining her health with drinking. She's had to look at how to tap into her creative self, which means doing some Eleventh Step work: seeking conscious contact with God "as we understood Him," asking for knowledge of God's will and the power to carry it out. Allie says, "It was a long time before I knew that that was what I needed to do. That I might one day be able to bring who I am into full flower is an idea I'm trying on for size. It's meant developing a patient awareness I never had before."

Her awareness has brought her to a new sense of accountability that many other people with three years of sobriety have also acquired.

Can I Really Do What I Want to Do?

"I've learned that life isn't just something that falls into your lap," Allie says. "You have to do some initiating. Believe me, this has not been a comfortable lesson. But there is some joy at the end."

Allie got by for most of her life on a fair amount of talent, but not much work. "I know a number of actors I went to school with as a kid who have great careers. They all looked up to me as the one who was going to make it. I was the star, the talented one, the girl who could play everyone from Peter Pan to Blanche Dubois at age twelve!" Allie laughs. "I *am* talented. I'm able to say that now, without bragging. But I also know that I've got lousy work habits, and I didn't put in the spadework other people did. I got by on chutzpah and luck and pulling the wool over a lot of eyes. It's hard to think of myself as anything but a con artist, even now, in sobriety. It's only been in the past few weeks that I've begun to think there might be hope."

Allie remembers how bad her last few years of drinking and drugging were. "I made such a fool of myself in auditions at the height—or maybe I should say the depths—of my drinking and drugging. Before that, I got on some TV shows. Walk-on parts, but with lines. Cocktail waitresses, younger sisters, this or that screaming woman in a crowd. Before I started getting regularly zonked out, I was getting a reputation as a versatile minor character. I was hardly a star, which of course bothered the hell out of me, and was why, I told myself, I drank and took downs. I was so mad at the world for not giving me instant acclaim. The madder I got, the more I got wasted, and the worse I looked and acted. Until, by the end . . ." Allie winces.

"You know, in L.A., it's all who you know—or at least that's the game I thought I had to play. So in the last couple of years, despite the fact that I really didn't know anybody, I'd rely on whatever Hollywood gossip I could squeeze out of my few remaining friends in the business, and try to present myself as this know-it-all, jaded sophisticate, talking about Steve Spielberg and Barbra and *when* were Dustin and Bob Redford going to do another movie together . . . blah, blah, blah. God, it's amazing that anybody put up with me. By the end, not many people did. I'd dress like some kind of neo-Marilyn Monroe—trying to outdo Madonna—which was not a pretty sight, especially in the last two years, when I couldn't hack the high heels and my face looked like a kindergarten art class had at it.

"I alienated so many people that I was barred from coming back to certain studios. But the worst part was, underneath the outrageous, grotesque clown I'd become, I knew—a part of me always knew, even when I was completely out of it—what a fool I was making of myself, *but I couldn't stop doing it.* It's like my self-destructiveness knew no bounds. It wasn't only the booze and the drugs, though God knows that was evidence enough that I was bent on doing myself in. It was how I felt about myself. Self-hatred doesn't begin to say it."

Allie says she has a pretty good idea about the psychological and possibly genetic origins of her alcoholism. "My parents were drunks who divorced when I was a baby, and I was brought up by a grandmother who made no secret of the fact that she resented it." But, she says, "I feel really distant about all that. I'm so burned out about blaming my lousy childhood on everything. It's just gotten boring. What can I do about it now? Toward the end of my drinking, I just blamed myself. Now that I'm sober, I'm no longer trying to snow anybody. At least not much. I lied all my life and sometimes I sort of *modify* my credentials today, but it's nothing like it used to be. And because I no longer look like a harlot—I've let my hair go from platinum back to its natural dark brown, and I keep my clothes on at auditions—nobody seems to recognize the old me, thank heavens. I'm not nearly as hurt by my reputation as I feared I would be. So I feel a little better about myself. At least I'm not acting like the monster I used to act like. But why can't I get anywhere now that I'm sober? What's holding me back?"

Allie says she shares all this in meetings, but she admits she hasn't allowed herself to get close to very many people in AA. "There are a lot of huge meetings in Los Angeles," she says. "Sometimes they feel like revival meetings—speakers using a mike at the podium, with an audience of three hundred adoring fans. Well, that's unfair, I'm modifying again. Meetings are fine, and actually there are plenty of smaller ones where you do get to speak if you want to. But, I don't know—I don't want to bore people. I'm so ashamed of how I used to dominate people when I drank and drugged, how obnoxious I was. I just want people to like me. I'm afraid to let out too many of all these negative feelings I have about myself. Who wants to hear me bitch about myself?"

Allie has gone through four sponsors. "All of them were perfectly nice women, but I just couldn't pick up the phone. And anyway, I'm always on the run, going from audition to audition, doing freelance secretarial work—I am simply not available. My last sponsor was a flight attendant, which meant she was gone even more than I was. There hasn't been anybody I've felt connected to, which I know is as much my doing as anybody else's. In fact, I've started going to a lot fewer meetings this past year. The gap between me and the program was getting pretty wide. It's great to be sober, but I've got a life to live. If I had an audition the same time as a meeting, the meeting got scrapped, not the audition."

At an audition a few weeks ago, Allie had an experience that she says jolted her. "I haven't been able to see my life in the same way since." She explains: "I was at a cattle call for a dish detergent commercial. They wanted the usual sunny, cheery young mother type, someone to ooh and aah over how many bubbles she got out of a teaspoon of dish liquid. A lot of women about my age were crammed into this hot waiting room. The casting director was late, and everyone felt pretty disgruntled. It was a little humiliating. The *egos* actors have. Anyway, the door suddenly slammed open and this outrageous, red-haired, overly made-up girl stormed in, marched up to the receptionist, and loudly demanded to be told who was in charge here. She informed the receptionist that she didn't have all day, that they should be honored she was even thinking of auditioning for this stupid commercial, and the sooner they got the formality of the audition over so she could get the job over with, the better. She was up for a very important movie role and—had the receptionist heard her?—she didn't have all day." Allie groaned. "The girl was drunk, at the stage where she still had control over her limbs, but not her mouth. I knew this state well, having gotten to precisely that point at so many auditions myself. It was excruciating. The women around me were tittering or huffing self-righteously or squirming in embarrassment for the girl—and I saw, from the other side of the fence, what it must have been like to watch *me* at my worst. She wouldn't shut up. She demanded twice to be seen immediately. The receptionist kept repeating in a sweet and calm manner that the casting director had not yet arrived but if she cared to fill out an application and take a seat to wait her turn, she was more than welcome. The redhead persisted, slamming her right fist on the receptionist's desk. Finally, the receptionist had had it. 'Miss,' she said, 'if you don't behave I'll call the guard and you'll be escorted out.' The redhead glared at her—and then burst into tears. 'You don't understand,' she wailed. 'I *need* this job.' The most embarrassing silence I've ever had to sit through came over the room. Then I recalled the silences that often surrounded my own drunken, drugged scenes."

Allie shudders. "It was all I could take. I got up and walked over to her, put my arm around her, and asked her to take a walk outside with me. She turned docile; she was crying softly, like a little girl. She could have been led anywhere by anybody. God, that was familiar to me too." Allie said she walked the girl out of the building to a courtyard with benches. "We sat down. And she just cried. She let it all out. How if she didn't get a job soon, she didn't know what she would do. Become a prostitute, probably. Her boyfriend had threatened her. Her parents wouldn't help her anymore. She had no friends. Someone owed her money. Someone promised her a job but hadn't come through. She wanted to go to Mexico, maybe, or back East to New York, where she'd get on Broadway. Yes, that was what she needed to do. Get into a

Broadway play. She's had enough of L.A. and the movie business. Bunch of shallow assholes. She was a real artist.

"It was all so familiar. It was like listening to myself. I could smell the alcohol on her breath, her clothes, coming from her pores—it's incredible how it saturates you. All I did was sit there holding her, letting her spill it all out. Then I told her, 'I understand.' She looked at me tearfully and blubbered, 'How could *you* understand? You're so calm. You're such a success. You probably get every job you try out for! When I walked into the room and saw you, I knew you were one of lucky ones. The ones who always get the break. I can tell the winners a mile a way. How would you know what it's like to be a loser?"

Allie says she wishes she could report that she successfully Twelve Stepped the girl on the spot. "I did say that I used to drink but that I'd managed to get help, and if she thought she had a problem with that, I'd love to take her to an AA meeting. It was awkward. She hadn't even mentioned the obvious fact that she was half-bombed, so I felt a little strange launching into it. I hoped that maybe this was the moment of readiness for her, that she'd jump at the chance to get help. Instead she jumped down my throat. She spat out, 'How dare you presume I have a drinking problem!' It was hard to understand the words, they were getting so slurred. I detected the presence of some downs, quaaludes probably. She stood up with as much dignity she could muster and wobbled away without a word, out of the courtyard and out of sight. That's the last I saw of her."

Allie says she continued to sit on the bench, feeling dazed. "I was so unnerved. It was a flashback to my former life, my former self. I knew exactly how she felt; I knew her shame, her self-hate, her pain, her terror. And I knew something even more amazing. I knew that the person she saw was the real me. I *was* a success. I could navigate the world without the pain and fear that assailed her every moment; something incredible had been lifted from me. I appreciated on a whole new level that I was sober. Suddenly, life seemed to have so much possibility. I can't explain it. Out of all this came an incredibly strong and central sense that I was now really all right, that I'm okay. As long as I don't drink, don't drug, and keep connecting with other sober, recovering people—which I've started doing with a new and very different enthusiasm these past three weeks—as long as I take that kind of basic care of myself, the sky's the limit. There's nothing I can't try for. Now, so far Woody Allen has *not* offered to build his next movie around my extraordinary presence, based on that stirring dog food commercial he saw me in a year ago. Nothing in my outer life has really changed yet, except that I've started going to meetings with a new feeling of purpose, and even enjoyment. But I know, somehow, that I'm headed in a wonderful direction. How could I not be, now that I'm really choosing to be *alive?* And somehow I know this is all going to put me where I need to be."

Allie admits this sounds vague, but the feeling she talks about is tremendously strong. "It's a kind of awed gratitude, but it's also joy. Joy that comes out of an incredible sadness, a feeling of complete empathy for that tortured redhead, whose life is so much like my own life was when drugs and alcohol had taken me over. I don't know how to explain this sense of joy that is as much at home with crying as it is with laughing." Allie shakes her head and smiles, a little embarrassed. "Am I making any sense at all? I feel alive. My life feels like it has meaning. Something shifted in me as a result of meeting that girl and reaching out to help her, even if she couldn't receive it. I feel released from depression. And I don't feel I've got to lie about myself anymore. What's there to lie about? For the moment, anyway. I feel just fine—in fact, completely successful—being exactly who I am. I see life as something to initiate as well as to receive. That's part of the miracle I'm feeling right now. Whether I have a wonderful career as an actor, get married and have kids, or decide to do something completely different—whatever it is will come out of three things: my desire to do it, my willingness to exert every bit of willpower I have in the service of that desire, and a complete willingness to turn the results of my actions over to God.

"Sobriety now seems like an adventure I initiate and receive. The Serenity Prayer has a deeper meaning than it ever had before. I feel like I understand it on a whole new level. It's teaching me to strive for a real balance, to ask for and then depend on guidance to teach me what I've got power over and what I don't. And, even though I don't have much outer success right now, I have a strong feeling that I've got more power than I realized to reach for and attain my dreams, as well as *less* power than I realized to control the outcome of any actions I take! There's so much I can do; there's so much I must wait to receive, that I can't force with my will."

Allie laughs, and apologizes: "All this from meeting a poor, drunken girl at an audition for a dish detergent commercial! But who knows why we're ready to understand things when we are? Maybe frustration and despair just build up to a point of release— or leap to the next level. I don't know. I only know that I wouldn't be feeling any of this hope if I hadn't stopped drinking and drugging. I'd be out there wobbling on high heels, getting kicked out of another audition, railing at the world for not being what I wanted it to be."

> *God grant me serenity to accept the things I cannot change;*
> *Courage to change the things I can;*
> *And wisdom to know the difference.*

Many people in their third year of sobriety have a new understanding of the wisdom in the Serenity Prayer. We see the causes and effects at work in our lives, and how much of what happens is a result of our actions and our attitudes. Accepting this accountability requires full, vigilant, conscious participation in our lives. And yet we need to appreciate just as completely what we *don't* have power over, and we need to turn it over.

Accepting that living a satisfying life in sobriety takes willpower, and turning it over opens us to new possibilities in life. A lot of people have found that they no longer need to see themselves in the old limited ways. Burt discovered that being the manager of an Italian restaurant was pretty satisfying, even if it was as far from acclaimed sculptor as he could imagine; the door is still completely open to him to become the artist he wants to be, as he lets his creative self grow at the rate it needs to grow. Dennis learned to accept that he *deserves* the success he is enjoying as a Hollywood screenwriter; he saw it as a confluence of willpower and turning it over. It was a tribute to his talent and hard work and timing, but it was also a gift, something that came to him because it was the right time for it to happen. Martha started to free herself from the backwater Louisiana town where she'd felt trapped, because she discovered a new capacity to forgive, to love, and to understand other people's pain.

The wisdom that these third-year recoverers have cultivated and shared with me has come through the acceptance of power and powerlessness, our potential and our limitations. If we'll just "wait for the miracle," the miracle will come.

In fact, the miracle already *has* come. Allie says, "Being sober teaches me that I'm all right just as I am." Being sober seems to mean that for the rest of us too. As we accept the responsibility, joy, and mystery of living life in full consciousness, the full consciousness of sobriety becomes its own reward.

You've Got to Give It
Away to Keep It

TO:

FROM:

Suggested Reading

The following books are all official "conference-approved" publications of Alcoholics Anonymous, published by AA World Services, Inc., and are available through AA and some bookstores:

Alcoholics Anonymous (The Big Book). 3d ed. New York: Alcoholics Anonymous World Services, Inc., 1976.

Twelve Steps and Twelve Traditions. New York: Alcoholics Anonymous World Services, Inc., 1981.

As Bill Sees It. New York: Alcoholics Anonymous World Services, Inc., 1967.

Living Sober. New York: Alcoholics Anonymous World Services, Inc., 1975.

Came to Believe. New York: Alcoholics Anonymous World Services, Inc., 1973.

In addition, I heartily recommend the following:

B., Hamilton. *Getting Started in AA.* Center City, Minn.: Hazelden, 1995.

————. *Twelve Step Sponsorship: How It Works.* Center City, Minn.: Hazelden, 1996.

B., Mel. *New Wine: The Spiritual Roots of the Twelve Step Miracle.* Center City, Minn.: Hazelden, 1991.

Carnes, Patrick. *A Gentle Path through the Twelve Steps.* Center City, Minn.: Hazelden, 1993.

————. *Out of the Shadows: Understanding Sexual Addiction.* Center City, Minn.: Hazelden, 1992.

————. *Sexual Anorexia: Overcoming Sexual Self-Hatred.* Center City, Minn.: Hazelden, 1997.

Gorski, Terence T. *Passages through Recovery.* Center City, Minn.: Hazelden, 1997.

Kettelhack, Guy. *Easing the Ache: Gay Men Recovering from Compulsive Behavior.* Center City, Minn.: Hazelden, 1998.

Kominars, Sheppard B., and Kathryn D. Kominars. *Accepting Ourselves and Others: A Journey into Recovery from Addictive and Compulsive Behaviors for Gays, Lesbians and Bisexuals.* Center City, Minn.: Hazelden, 1996.

Kurtz, Ernest. *Not-God: A History of Alcoholics Anonymous.* Center City, Minn.: Hazelden, 1991.

Levine, Stephen. *A Gradual Awakening.* New York: Anchor Books, 1989.

Larsen, Earnie. *Stage II Recovery: Life Beyond Addiction.* San Francisco: HarperSanFrancisco, 1985.

————. *Stage II Relationships: Love Beyond Addiction.* San Francisco: HarperSanFrancisco, 1987.

Martin, John. *Blessed Are the Addicts: The Spiritual Side of Alcoholism, Addiction and Recovery.* New York: Villard, 1991.

SUGGESTED READING · 131

Narcotics Anonymous. 5th ed. Van Nuys, Calif.: Narcotics Anonymous World Service Office, Inc., 1988.

Schaeffer, Brenda. *Is It Love or Is It Addiction?* Center City, Minn.: Hazelden, 1997.

Z., Phillip. *A Skeptic's Guide to the Twelve Steps.* Center City, Minn.: Hazelden, 1991.

About the Author

Guy Kettelhack is the author or co-author of more than a dozen nonfiction books, including

First-Year Sobriety: When All That Changes Is Everything

Second-Year Sobriety: Getting Comfortable Now That Everything Is Different

Easing the Ache: Gay Men Recovering from Compulsive Behaviors

Sober and Free: Making Your Recovery Work for You

On a Clear Day You Can See Yourself, with Dr. Sonya Friedman

Love Triangles, with Dr. Bonnie Jacobson

Dancing around the Volcano